BUILDING WITH STONE

BUILDING WITH STONE

by Charles McRaven

Illustrations by
Chandis Ingenthron and the author
Photographs by
Linda Moore McRaven and the author

A GARDEN WAY PUBLISHING BOOK

STOREY COMMUNICATIONS, INC.
POWNAL, VERMONT 05261

For Lauren
sunshine upon stones

Text design by Linda Moore McRaven
Cover design by Mallory Lake
Front cover photograph by Steve Swinburne
Back cover photographs by Steve Swinburne
  (top and bottom) and Don Paulson (center)
Typesetting by Accura Type & Design

Printed in the United States by The Alpine Press

Second printing, January 1990

Library of Congress Cataloging-in-Publication Data
McRaven, Charles
   Building with stone / Charles McRaven; illustrations by Chandis Ingenthron and the author; photographs by Linda Moore McRaven and the author.
      p.   cm.
   Reprint. Originally published: New York : Lippincott & Crowell, c1980.
   "A Garden Way Publishing book."
   Includes index.
   ISBN 0-88266-550-2 :
   ISBN 0-88266-569-3 (hc)
   1. Building, Stone—Amateurs' manuals.   I. Title.
[TA676.M32   1989]
693'.1—dc19

TABLE OF CONTENTS

Fallen fireplace chimney of ledge sandstone, north branch of Roark Creek, Taney
County, Missouri. House type unknown;
date unknown; builder unknown.

THE STONES REMAIN

MY DOG AND I walked the long slopes upcreek from our log house, savoring the last sunlight of first April after a bitter winter and uncertain spring. This is ledge-rock country, limestone-ribbed with scatterings of thin sandstone at certain heights on the slopes; glade country, with a skin of soil over the gray mass of stone, gnarled post oak clumping the hillsides, and thickets devouring the soil along the wet-weather streams.

We found the toppled chimney of a settler's cabin, its drystone ledge sandstone fallen in over the space the house had occupied. No trace of hewn log or beam, of board or nail, and only the barest outline of foundation cornerstones, moss-grown and sunken. Most significant, no dump of old cans or broken glass. This cabin fell at a time when nothing was thrown away.

A half acre of benchland soil above the creek branch had once been cleared where 18-inch-diameter cedars now towered. No fence—it would have been split rails, long decayed or burned in a woods fire. Up from the fallen stones led the faint trace of a steep wagon road, with stones stacked out of it. No rubber tires could negotiate this hill; it wound up to a limestone ledge and followed around a side draw to climb eventually to join the old stagecoach road above, itself unused for a hundred years. He would have walked mostly, this pioneer, maybe ridden; in most places the track was far too narrow for any wheels.

Seldom is a pioneer homestead so completely erased. We poked around and found a long double row of stones against the hill—caved-in root cellar or smokehouse lower level, both structures vital in the new country. Below the house, in the side draw, wet now with thaw, we found the spring, the precious trickle that made life among the parched glades in the dry rattle of summer possible. The side stream, the branch itself, goes dry before July, even at my house a half mile below. This spring must be, or must have been, year-round.

And there are the few stacked stones, heavy in moss, that outline the springhouse. The spring was rocked up to form a pool just within the foundation, but the soil around it has caved in and moved back into the hill. Now only these few stones remain, with the faint song of the trickling water. A path dents the rise to the cabin site, and another across the side draw. That way still lies the little old house that served as a stage stop far up the ridge. Springs are and were few in this country; dimly in my mind those forgotten settlers move up the path, laden with wooden buckets in an ongoing task we could not live with today.

Over in the woods is another square outline of stones. Barn-size, it was the small shed barn of the hills, for the horse and maybe a milk cow. Again no wood, no iron. There would have been hog pens, and up the slope is the telltale level spot the rooting and the mud produce. No stones here; the long-ago mud seals everything. Old-timers say the one sure way to keep a pond from leaking is to pen hogs in it for a few months and then just sort of wait for the smell to go away.

In this book, I tell you about ponds and stone dams, about barns of stone and stone springhouses and root cellars, about houses of stone, and about fireplace chimneys like the one we visited this day—how to build them, how and why. It is gratifying work, but not easy. Like all crafts, stonework demands a lot of you in patience, in labor, and in art.

Last week I built a stone arch as part of a de-modernizing restoration of a seventy-year-old building we own, the project shown in photographs in Chapter Nineteen. Before I could leave it for the night, propped up on its iron-rod temporary bracing, I had to set the keystone, or a child could knock out a prop and a ton of stone would cascade down on him. So I stayed at it until midnight, then slept in my Land Rover a sidewalk away, to finish it the next day.

That arch will long outlive me, and since the building is a National Historic Landmark, it should be intact for many generations. That's what building with stone is all about: time. Time needed to put together this oldest and most durable of materials and have the structure stand for as long as anything stands in this world. My own house has a lot of stone in it, and some trace of it will stand far into the future, come fire or decay.

That may be what this settler thought, and now his stones are scattered and grown over and gone back into the earth. I could probably find out from county records who he was and when he lived here. Was he a lone hunter, grubbing a corn patch along the creek, or did he raise a family here in this lost hollow? I don't really want to know a name: He is the hands that set these stones one upon the other in a sparse and ungiving land before my century was new.

No one living near knows of a cabin site here. They speak of others long vanished, of a small mill dam downcreek, washed out now, and traces of old roads and creek fords and meetinghouses. Nothing is left of this man who set his house among the forest.

Nothing but the stones.

Roark Creek
Taney County, Missouri
April 1979

IT IS TEN YEARS LATER NOW, as we prepare the second edition of this book, with more photographs and more information. We have laid a great deal of stone in those ten years, in many parts of the country. There has been Kentucky bluestone and Tennessee lime rock; Virginia granite and greenstone and slate; white and brown West Virginia sandstone and the black Shenandoah limestone that weathers almost white, squared first by German settlers when the country was young.

We're shaping more stone now, for the tighter joints popular today, still using hammers and chisels of my forging. It takes about as long to search for that "right rock" as it does to help one along with stone cutting. I still like the aged surfaces best, weathered and lichened and incredibly old.

We are restoring and building houses in Central Virginia now, of stone and old logs and beams, houses that look as if they are a hundred and fifty years old when we're finished. We do a lot of fireplaces and chimneys, and some stone veneer, but our basic work is solid stone. Big stones, some we have to handle with hydraulic power or winch cable. Stones that stand bold in their strength.

You will discover a phenomenon in setting a stone well. It slips into place when it is right, and immediately becomes rigid, finding, with your help, the place it has sought for its millions of years. It begins a new life now, part of a whole, of your contribution to good building, the work of your hands. Of your art.

Albemarle County, Virginia
January, 1989

This drystone wall ranges over and across hills in Stone County, Arkansas, in long sweeps that attest to its builders' labor and dedication to clearing the mountain fields. Details on page 35.

Figure 1-1. Our house in Virginia shows the use of stone as timeless, maintenance-free material, adaptable to almost any architecture and period.

CHAPTER ONE

STONE AS A BUILDING MATERIAL

IN THE COURSE of your building projects you will sooner or later come to the use of stone, the oldest, most durable, and certainly one of the most beautiful materials. Stone is often misused, which probably means that it's misunderstood. It has certain design limitations and requirements, certain structural characteristics, certain overall uses. There are certainly some building applications for which stone is totally wrong, for one or more reasons. We'll talk first about some of its general characteristics.

Compared with other building materials, stone is expensive if you count your time, cheap if you don't. It's heavy, but also permanent. It's bad insulation, but it makes a tight wall that radiates stored heat for hours. It does not make a strong wall unless the wall is very thick, and it depends mostly on its weight for stability. The most natural of materials, stone can grace almost any monstrosity you want to build with its landscape-blending appearance.

Of course, you can foul it up, but learning to build with natural stone is less demanding than learning to build with most other materials—that is, if you proceed with liberal doses of common sense and care. Even your early efforts will afford you a great degree of satisfaction when you view the structures of plywood and plastic around you.

Stone weighs more than anything you'll build with except steel and concrete. You'll handle each rock several times in gathering, hauling, stacking, shaping, and laying it. This weight will mean you need stronger footings and more carefully fitted arches and spans. But this weight will also keep what you build where you build it, against great odds.

Here is a chart showing some relative weights and other characteristics of common stone:

TYPE	WEIGHT	WORKABILITY	STRENGTH
soft sandstone	light	easy	low
dense sandstone	medium	medium	medium to high
limestone	heavy	medium to hard	medium to high
granite	heavy	hardest	high
slate	medium	easy	low
clay shale	medium	easy	low
basalt	heavy	medium to hard	medium to high

We'll be discussing building with fieldstone primarily—stone lying on top of the ground as opposed to stone freshly quarried. It can be any of those listed, or others, such as gneiss or even marble.

I prefer dense sandstone but have worked with coarse or crumbly sandstone, limestone, granite, chert, and some other rocks I wasn't sure about.

I use the stronger stones—limestone and granite—for things like bridge spans and stone lintels, for obvious reasons. Soft or weak stone has little shear strength and must always be supported. Laid properly, however, even crumbly stone will let you build well. That means you use to advantage the downward and side thrusts of the stone's weight, balancing it against itself in arches and against fill dirt in retaining walls, cushioning it in mortar for maximum crush strength.

Our fireplaces are both in a chimney of very soft white sandstone, weathered a gray brown and picked up on our hillside. I was able to shape the odd pieces with nothing more than the edge of my trowel while laying it up. Yet the 20-foot-plus column has not settled or cracked in its five years of use.

I will confess to a certain laziness in using this lighter sandstone, when all about our land and in our creekbed was good, dense limestone that was stronger (it was heavier, too). But sandstone is easier to shape than granite or limestone. Also, lichens grow better on the porous sandstone, and the chimney looks as if it has been there a long time.

Any stone is easier to work if it's fresh from the ground. Rural masons in my area used to work out the layered sandstone from under their fields with axes. It dried out hard, to be used for a variety of building needs, even some quite impressive chimneys. Masons refer to this ground water in stone as "sap," and try to use a stone before it dries.

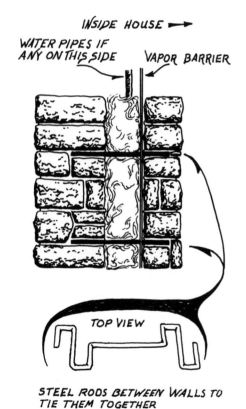

INSIDE HOUSE ➡

WATER PIPES IF ANY ON THIS SIDE

VAPOR BARRIER

TOP VIEW

STEEL RODS BETWEEN WALLS TO TIE THEM TOGETHER

Figure 1-2. For use in house construction, stone should be insulated and vapor-sealed to prevent "sweating." One answer is a double wall, tied together, with insulation and plastic sheeting between, on the interior side.

INSULATION

As insulation material, stone is poor. Stone houses and barns were often built with the idea that they would be warm, but heat flows right through the walls. But it was easier to stop drafts with a stone wall than with wood that shrank and swelled constantly, so our pioneer forebears used stone a lot.

I've had arguments with folks who've built well houses of stone, with no insulation, who claim the stone holds the heat better than wood. What they have is a column of earth-heated air that constantly comes up from the well and is trapped or slowed by the well house. Insulation would increase the efficiency much more.

For dwelling houses, two walls of stone with insulation between works well (Figs. 1-2, 1-3). Just one wall would be cold and would sweat with humidity and heat changes, but two, with the trapped air held immobile by insulation, is ideal. Of course it means twice the work, and the two walls should be tied together here and there for

Figure 1-3. Our kitchen wing is post-and-beam construction with stone fill inside, an insulated 2x4-framed midwall, and stone veneer outside, for a 14-inch thickness.

strength. Simply leaving a dead-air space between the walls doesn't work, because heat can convect via the circulated air. Insulation traps tiny bits of air and stops this circulation.

A stone house may be built with no insulation at all except overhead, where it's most useful. You'd get a tight structure and could probably live with the cost of heating it if you cut your own wood and had plenty of it. But there's still the moisture problem.

Another solution is a stud wall inside the heavy stone exterior wall, with insulation and conventional covering. I don't recommend the current practice of facing a stud-wall structure with thin stone that would not stand alone. Any minor disaster could bring its weight down, along with the rest of the house.

Stone should always be laid for strength as well as for beauty. To this end, it's never good design to have tall, thin columns of stone supporting, say, a porch roof. By its nature, this material demands a structure of visual mass. That same roof could be supported properly by heavy columns more like sections of stone wall or by stone arches with more mass than opening.

Now about that moisture problem. I recall a stone-walled, stone-floored house I lived in one year that had no vapor barrier or insulation. My shoes would turn green if I left them on the floor more than three days. You see, stone acts like a lamp wick to absorb moisture from the ground, and with heat inside and cold outside, a stone wall is like a windowpane; it actually mists over from the moisture in the air and sweats.

We have a vapor barrier under the flagstone floor of our hewn-log house, and nothing turns green on it. But I've never gotten around to insulating one stone wall of our kitchen lean-to, and it sweats all winter and chills that part of the room. My shoes would turn green on it, I know.

GET ENOUGH STONE

You'll need a good supply if you contemplate doing much stone-work. A little simple math will tell you that there are lots of stones in a wall of any size, and you'll be dismayed at just how much rock it takes to build something. I suggest you start small, with stone steps or a low wall, to get the feel of it.

If you have stone all over your land, so much the better, but if not, better figure some costs in getting it from elsewhere to here. In Chapter Two, on acquiring stone, we talk more about the problem, but don't make the mistake of thinking stone is free. Just transporting it can mean anything from the cost of a wheelbarrow to the cost of a hernia.

It's good to have lots of help, too. My neighbor, G.K. Land, was building the downhill mortared wall for his A-frame house eight years ago, more or less with my assistance (Fig. 1-4). We had several helpers carrying stone from the creekbed below: his wife and teenage children, and students from the nearby college where he, his wife, and I all worked. One of these students was a husky blonde girl who was setting a pace none of us could match.

We kept stumbling over a really big rock in searching out more usable ones, and all of us had remarked that it would sure build a lot of wall, wouldn't it? It was as long as I was, dense limestone, thicker than the 12-inch wall, and weighing at least 500 pounds. Not only was it huge, but the path from it led straight up the bank to the foundation wall, steep and narrow.

We eventually got all psyched up to get this big rock, and five of us managed to surround it. I was on the tail end with the big blonde, who was enjoying the whole thing. We got the rock up out of the gravel, all right, and got it moving toward the bank. Then the folks in front stepped up the bank and all the weight came back on us.

"Ugh," I said, my bird legs trembling and my eyes popping.

"Heavy?" the blonde asked.

"Ugh."

So she grinned, got a better grip, and lifted even more. I swear my feet came up off the ground. We were up the bank in no time, and the stone was set into its bed of mortar.

What a girl. I hope she's off building walls on her own homestead now, somewhere she's really appreciated.

Stone picked up from the woods, fields, or creekbeds always has a nice aged look, so when I lay it I try to keep weathered surfaces to the outside, doing whatever shaping is necessary where it won't show. We have the date '74 in our fireplace chimney slab, and more than one visitor has thought it's a hundred years older than it is.

I cannot emphasize enough that building with stone is a craft to be undertaken by degrees, learning as you go. And you must go slowly. Aside from being hard, dirty, and often dangerous work, constant demands are made on your judgment, common sense, and artistic abilities. A brick is a brick is a brick, but one stone isn't like any other stone in the world; each is its own challenge. You'll spend a lot of time trying and rejecting stones from your supply pile before

you find the right one for every spot. Often you'll have to make it fit by shaping it with a hammer and chisels or by using two instead of one.

You'll learn early that a 6x10x12-inch space in a mortared wall will not accept a 6x10x12-inch stone, with allowances made for the mortar joint. And you'll learn to eyeball sizes and shapes.

A critic of my hewn-log house-building procedures—all hand work—once observed that the object seemed to be to utilize a lot of technology to get the things thrown off by non-level, non-straight, non-vertical logs and log walls to come out even again. That's sort of the way building with stone is. Rare is the blocklike stone; most stones defy simple physics. So putting them up in useful, permanent, and beautiful structures despite their shapes will take a lot out of you.

And give a lot of satisfaction in return.

Figure 1-4. Part of G.K. Land's house foundation wall, showing the 6-foot slab of creek limestone it took five of us to carry.

Figure 2-1. Often a prime source for
stone, walls and chimneys from fallen or
burned houses consist of the best stones
the original builders gathered.

ACQUIRING STONE

BEFORE YOU CREATE your stone wall, span your first arch, or raise your stone house any place but in your imagination, you first have to get your hands on the stuff.

I have recycled stone walls, fireplace chimneys, dams, and foundations for material. I have raided roadside ditches and streambeds and farmers' fields. I have scoured the woods for just the lichened specimens I needed, and I've bartered in the best used-car tradition for coveted prime stone wherever it might be.

Upon occasion, I've been invited to return stones I was in the act of acquiring, but this was early in my masonry career. More recently I've had success convincing farmers that, say, the 300 square feet of stone I wanted from their pasture was at that instant preventing 300 square feet of grass from growing. It should be removed immediately—if not for free, at least for a piddling sum. Beware the shrewd Yankee farmer who may compute the area of grass crushed by your tire tracks into the bargain.

Ideally, the real estate you've bought has usable stone on it, if not all over it. And just about any stone is usable for *something*, even if it must be cut, shaped, or held in place temporarily with forms to get it into a wall, steps, or a barbecue pit.

Assume you do have rocks on your acreage or lot. Much of the land available now is the leftover corners too stony to farm by our forebears, so it's often a safe assumption.

First of all, look over the stones to see what you'll be able to do with them. Let's hope you have some that are reasonably flat on top and bottom, whatever else their topography. That makes them easier to lay, no matter what pattern or style you use. Given round stones of New England granite or really grotesque chunks lacking any flat sides, your job is proportionately harder. We'll discuss shapes and pattern more later.

GO PROSPECTING

I take along a short prybar, or crowbar, to pry stones up for a better look. An innocent plane surface can belie a distorted shape belowground—sometimes way below. Flip over a few dozen to get an idea of the characteristics of your stones. In a given area, rocks tend to reflect the shapes their formative strata gave them, so a nice 4-inch-thick ledge could produce lots of 4-inch stones of varying other dimen-

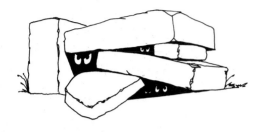

Figure 2-2. Stones are the shelter for countless creatures, many of whom are not benign. Care should always be taken when gathering.

sions. A few million years' wear will round, chip, or otherwise disguise this basic shape, but there will still be similarities. If you find a few good ones, keep digging around. There'll be more.

Be prepared to step nimbly back if you discover the inevitable snake, spider, ants, or wasps underneath. And wear gloves—the thick leather kind.

When building my blacksmith shop in the town near us, I had made a habit of scaling a nearby deserted hill in my Land Rover for stone each morning. One day I'd forgotten both my prybar and my gloves—but what the hell, stonemasons are tough. So are blacksmiths, right? I collected several stones, then lifted one from a loose pile. A wasp from a small but obviously closeknit family nest underneath stung my hand before I could drop the rock and disappear over the horizon. Unlike a bee, a wasp stings repeatedly, and this one had reinforcements.

That's when I should have quit, but I didn't. I decided I was still far from a full load, so I gritted my teeth and went on—at a respectable distance from the rock pile.

Three stones later I turned one up and felt fresh pain sear my already throbbing hand. A scorpion. But there were two benefits from the experience: I forgot all about the wasp sting and realized my Land Rover was loaded full, after all.

MOVING STONES

Picking up rocks is hard work. The higher you lift them and the farther you walk with them, the harder you work. A device that has been around for centuries is the stoneboat, a simple sled very near the ground (Fig. 2-3). Large stones can be rolled or tumbled onto it (Fig. 2-4); small ones need be lifted a shorter distance. It's best shod with steel runners, to make it easier to pull with tractor, mule, automobile,

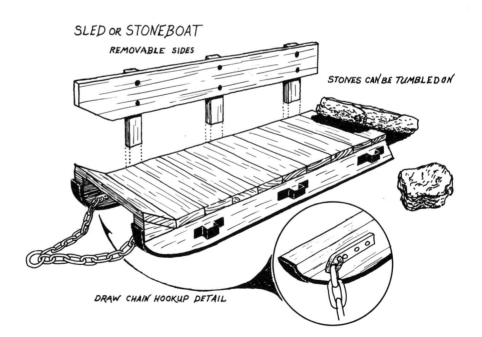

SLED OR STONEBOAT
REMOVABLE SIDES
STONES CAN BE TUMBLED ON
DRAW CHAIN HOOKUP DETAIL

Figure 2-3. The stoneboat is a strong, low sled for transporting stones without having to lift them. It can have sides and should have steel runners.

Figure 2-4. Sometimes rolling a stone is the best way to move it, as in this picture from a chimney restoration in central Virginia. The stone was pried up and rounds of firewood slipped under.

four-wheel-drive, or people power. Pulled down a steep hill, it can and will run over or under you, however. The only escape seems to be increasing speed to stay out of the way, which makes for some pretty spectacular stone hauls. An automotive towbar-type hitch will help solve this problem.

Another handy vehicle is the farm cart or two-wheeled trailer, pulled by the same motive power. I advise against moving it by hand when loaded, because it will *always* run over you. Pneumatic automotive tires and wheels make the modern cart easier to pull around and let you use it on the highways.

A pickup truck is quite handy around any sort of job site, but you may not be able to justify owning one in your situation. Make friends with one, swap labor—something can always be worked out.

For short distances, a wheelbarrow is still probably the best conveyor. You'll need one anyway for sand and probably for use as a mixing box. Don't get a toy with thin pipe handles and a wheel off a baby carriage. It should have an oak frame, a heavy steel box, and a pneumatic tire. It will cost you a bundle but, properly cared for, will haul many tons and outlast your lifetime.

This is as good a place as any to tell you how to load a wheelbarrow. Put most of the weight back near the handles, not over the wheel. True, you lift more, but you'll find you can actually control the thing, which you cannot possibly do with the wheel burying itself in the ground while you strain to direct the gyrating handles. And those clever garden carts with two bicycle wheels are fine for concrete surfaces, but I wouldn't move rocks from their natural habitat in one.

In the woods or on soft ground, forget even the wheelbarrow and go it by hand. Try to minimize the carrying distance by positioning your vehicle among the stones, being careful to avoid soft places. A pickup truck full of rocks is harder to unstick than an empty one, once it's really in deep.

When lifting heavy objects, you must keep your back straight and give your knees and legs the workout (Fig. 2-5). It's awkward at first, but absolutely necessary. Nothing is as unyielding as stone, and you don't want to have to enjoy your finished structure from a wheelchair. Get into moving stones gradually, and do a lot of toe-touching exercises to head off that lower-back ache.

Figure 2-5. Proper lifting stance involves bending your knees to let your legs do the work, not your back. The stone in the background was handled with the hydraulic bucket on the tractor.

DON'T OVERLOAD

Once loaded, your pickup truck or trailer or sled will be hard to manage. You could compute the weight as you load if you're good at guessing; then you'd know when to stop loading. But make the first load a light one—you can add more as you get the feel for it. A load of stone isn't as hard to get going as it is to get stopped.

Sometimes you just can't get stopped. I once contracted to do stone veneer on a large Boy Scout camp mess hall in the mountains of Arkansas, and I hired some half-wild teenagers to help. An itinerant preacher of some obscure faith was also doing some carpentry at the camp with his crew, and one day one of my boys turned up a stone with a ground snake under it. The preacher went crazy, screaming at us to torture that creature of the devil, chop it into bits, burn it.

So of course these fun-loving boys, sensing a good ongoing joke, began collecting the harmless king snakes, bull snakes, and garter snakes we ran into every day in collecting stone. They'd appear mysteriously in the preacher's lunch box, in his sleeping bag, under his hat. He always gave a howling performance.

One day we were loading stone onto the ancient surplus flatbed truck the camp had provided, high up a nightmare-steep mountainside—the kind that means you have somebody block the wheels of the vehicle before you trust low gear and the hand brake to hold you stationary, even empty. And we weren't empty. This job took lots of stone and we had thousands of pounds on, nearly ready for the plunge down the mountain.

Then one of the boys found a large blacksnake and stashed it in the glove compartment for preacher-baiting. When we were ready, I insisted the boys take their pet out. If the compartment door bounced open, I couldn't guarantee how well I'd control the truck with all that writhing help. They could keep it back on the truckbed, where they rode (to make it easier to leap to safety when the truck finally ran amuck). So we opened the compartment. No snake. Got out of a crack somewhere.

I made those boys take the seat out and search every inch of the truck cab. No snake. Guess he went out an open window. Okay. Reassemble the cab. Climb back in. Start engine. With my foot on the brake, I eased the monster load out onto the steep road. The nose dropped out of sight as the engine peaked in first gear.

This hill was so steep I was looking down standing tree trunks. I glanced up, and not six inches from my forehead was five feet of coiled snake on the tilted sun visor, flicking its forked tongue at me.

Blacksnakes are harmless. Harmless. I told myself that at least a thousand times between wondering which jolt would tip the visor and dump it onto me.

Couldn't stop the truck. Couldn't abandon it via door or window with my own and three other lives at stake. (Or could I? Those other three were rapidly losing value in my mind.)

Well, I rode it all down to a relatively level spot, stopped the truck gently, set the brake, turned off the ignition, and without opening the door I cleared the open window at a roar with that snake reflex, which propels in defiance of natural laws. Then I blued the air, withering greenery and the ears of those kids, ending both their snake pranks and my overloading the truck with stone.

HANDLE WITH CARE

In loading, try to stack thin stones on edge, so the weight and bouncing won't break them. Wedge them tightly to keep them from dominoing on a curve of the road going home (Fig. 2-6). Always have sides on for whatever you haul, at any speed. I hate to think of the liability of depositing a large rock through the hood or the windshield of a car behind you.

Don't drop or throw stones onto each other. Your choice material can become a pile of rubble, especially if it's soft sandstone.

Always collect more stone than you could possibly need. If you're bargaining for stone, leave the option of an extra load or two. If you don't actually use it on the planned project, you'll discover laying stone is such fun you'll want to build something else.

Don't steal stone. It's unreasonable to assume the owner doesn't want it or doesn't intend to use it for something. If he'll sell, the purchase price is usually modest, against the cost in time, labor, and money for transporting it. (The actual cost should be whatever you're willing to pay. Ask around and find out the going rate.) Don't tear down a rural stone wall or fence without permission. They are invariably beautiful just where they are, a testimony to the labor of years the farmer invested to keep his fields clear. Unless you're damn good, you won't be able to re-create anything as beautiful or as meaningful.

Besides, you'll get caught. I particularly like the story of the president of the small college where I taught near here. He'd "come by" some very nice cut limestone many years ago and had it hauled to his rural property, planning to build a house there eventually.

Years went by. The school grew and so did his duties. The house had to be put off. By now he had to have a CB radio, telephone, and other gadgets installed in his Lincoln to keep track of things. Meanwhile, grass grew up around the stone and cattle grazed there.

Then one day, he and his wife visited the site to plan the house and discovered a local there, loading his pickup truck with their stone. Well, the fellow was cool. He sized up this well-dressed couple as probably not even the real owners of the land—what with the cows and all—and never slackened his loading pace as he greeted them.

"Just getting some of this rock out of the way."

"You have any idea who this belongs to?" the president asked.

"Well, it's been laying here for as long as I can remember. Don't look like anybody's got plans fer it." Still loading.

"Well, it's mine, and it just happens I do have plans for it."

"Oh. Well, then, I'll just take this one load, bein's it's all loaded up." He looked around ruefully at the rest of the stone.

FLAT STONES STACKED ON EDGE

Figure 2-6. Load flagstone or thin stones on edge, wedging them to keep them from falling. If laid flat in trailer or truck, bouncing will shatter them.

"No, you won't. You put every one back, right now!"

The man looked hurt. "Now, you wouldn't grudge a man a few rocks, would you?" He edged toward his open truck door.

So the president just reached into his car, took out his CB microphone, and began to summon the sheriff. He didn't have time to complete the call before the stone was all back on the ground and the rustic mason only a cloud of dust.

Suffice it to say that if you had bought, collected, hauled, and stacked a supply, you too would be irritated to find it gone on the day you wrangled free to begin construction. Stones are not quite like weeds; not everyone wants them removed.

RECYCLE

Recycled foundations are good sources for stone. Galloping progress is consuming older houses to make way for the wonders of discount stores and taco hells. House-wrecking crews will often bulldoze the stone, since it's heavy, expensive in time and labor to move, and dubiously salable at a profit. If you're there at the right time with a trailer and large prybar, you can often get prime stone free. Work on weekends or evenings; no construction or destruction crew can have a zealous scavenger underfoot.

SAFETY AND LIABILITY

If you drop a rock on your foot, just grimace and bear it. You will become an unknown and clumsy trespasser, no matter whose permission you once had, if you contemplate anybody else's liability.

Which reminds me to remind you always to be careful. Gloves don't preclude a smashed finger; steel-toed boots don't keep rocks off ankles; safety goggles don't keep flying rock chips from shearing off part of your nose.

Messing around with stone is a lot like mountain climbing or kayaking whitewater—nature barely tolerates you if you're extremely careful. I could have been smashed against a tree even without that snake in the truck. Once while prospecting a cliff face I took a step the wrong way and fell, rolled, and slid the equivalent of fifteen stories to land face down among—and covered by—my beloved rocks. Smarted.

You will find snakes under rocks and in rock piles. Cool there. Bugs there to eat. Here in the United States, we have only the copperhead, rattlesnake, moccasin, and, in the lowland South, the coral snake to fear. These are readily identifiable, but you and I will continue to flee first and conjecture later. Look for the copperhead and rattlesnake under rocks, and don't trust anything with a thin neck and large, triangular head.

I seldom dispatch a poisonous snake unless it's in residence close to home and children, and never a nonpoisonous one. Good rodent eaters. A friend recently decided to move a copperhead off into the woods, but he did a clumsy job of catching it and was bitten. He reacted to the antivenin and was very sick. Sometimes nature doesn't even tolerate you.

Just remember that rocks and snakes go together, and watch it. So do rocks and black widow spiders, wasps, and other irritating fauna.

OTHER SOURCES

A couple of other stone-gathering examples in parting: Houses were being demolished in the town near our home to make way for the inevitable highway. I needed stone for our house foundation but had been too busy to go haggle with the house wreckers—individuals, in this case—until only one grand old house with a substantial stone foundation remained.

I waited for demolition to begin, checking every afternoon or so. Nothing. Then one day, the house wasn't there any more. Some folks had bought it and had it moved and set on concrete blocks. What was left were foundation walls and a basement lined with quarried limestone, which just matched the work I'd begun.

By then the road contractor's bulldozers were revving their engines. It was close work for me each afternoon till dark, but our house sits atop five feet of those stones today.

Another time I began an arched-stone addition to an English half-timber building we owned in town, but I soon ran out of bartered stone. One day a lad who'd cleaned up a house demolition site appeared with a large trailerload of good stone, knowing I'd need it. I knew he'd need his trailer unloaded soon, too, so we did some close trading. He now owns a set of hand-forged chisels and punches for the lot, delivered and stacked.

Other times I have not been so fortunate. One summer I built a fireplace chimney and house foundation with stone hauled 110 miles by pickup truck at great expense—I was paying the collector/hauler a good wage—only to discover later a freak deposit of just the right kind of sandstone among the lime rock of a wooded hillside not a quarter mile away.

Don't try to use mossy stone with mortar—moss will die. Lichens are delicate too, so you have to keep the cement away from them. Ground moisture lets these organisms grow, and except for accent stones in your garden, you won't be able to duplicate the habitat.

You may avoid all the pitfalls of gathering stone simply by buying it and having it hauled and deposited. But getting it yourself will whet your anticipation for the actual construction. You'll get your back and legs in shape. And most important, you'll be able to choose the rocks you're to use on your wall, house, bridge, or fireplace.

And you'll probably have lots of funny stories to tell, later.

Figure 3-1. Shaping stone with hammer and chisel, mason Daniel Smith uses the cured wall of the stone porch for a table. The arched space beneath was for wood storage.

CHAPTER THREE

TOOLS FOR STONE

STONE IS our oldest building material, and the tools for working with it are almost as old. They've evolved from simple sticks and other pieces of stone to some still simple but effective hand tools that let you master the substance.

For gathering stone I use two prybars more than any other tools. One is a light, 3-foot bar I forged from automotive coil spring about ¾ inch thick. It has a hardened chisel point, and the rest is tempered for toughness. It's the bar I use to turn up stones in the woods and fields and along old fencerows to see what kinds of surprises are underneath. It will also shear off an offending protrusion on soft stone or lever a heavy stone into place.

The other bar is a 30-pound, 5-foot one of similar design used mainly for demolishing old mortared walls. It's actually a digging bar, for use in punching through subterranean rock formations, but its other applications are many. If a stone cannot be levered with this tool, you don't want any part of it anyway. A large, clearly grained specimen can often be split into manageable halves with the big bar. A few well-placed blows across the face of a large stone with the chisel point will often sunder it nicely, too. In short, this tool is for the heavy stuff.

MOVING THEM

Getting the stone home means using one or more of the devices we talked about last chapter: wheelbarrow, stoneboat, trailer, or truck. Getting it into or onto the conveyance is usually a matter of handwork. The stoneboat requires little or no lifting but is limited in range.

I have been fortunate enough to have the use of such devices as a front loader, boom, powered winch, and hand winch in loading stone. These are nice for large stones or stone in large quantities. For your average weekend project, you can usually handle the job by hand.

The ratchet hoist, or "come-along," is handy for big stones such as fireplace lintels (Fig. 3-2). You can set up a simple tripod of 2x4s or poles over the stone, chained together at the top, with another chain around the stone. Keep the legs of the tripod far enough apart to back your trailer or pickup truck between them after the stone is in the air. These hoists will handle half a ton easily, and you won't want any stones that heavy.

Big stuff can also be slid up a wide, thick plank with the come-along,

Figure 3-2. I'm using a ratchet hoist ("come along") to lift stone for this chimney in Southwest Missouri.

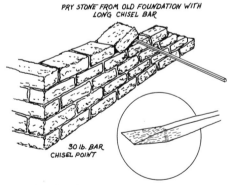

PRY STONE FROM OLD FOUNDATION WITH
LONG CHISEL BAR

30 lb. BAR
CHISEL POINT

Figure 3-3. A handy tool for stone gathering is this sharpened digging bar. It is useful both for prying up stones from the ground and for taking apart old walls for recycled material.

by hand, or inched up with the small prybar (Fig. 3-3). A 2x12-inch piece of sound oak will support 300 to 400 pounds, but the softer woods like pine or spruce are not for this kind of work. (An old bulldozer operator I knew always kept a pair of 4-inch-thick loading planks made of "red ellum" for his rig.) Always have help when you load large stones, if for no other reason than to dig you out from under whatever might fall on you.

For really heavy rocks, I use an A-frame ("gin poles") on the front of my Land Rover, with the winch cable up through a sheave and down (Fig. 3-5). This is for the stone that will, say, span a brook completely or form the lintel of an 8-foot fireplace or anchor a small dam.

If you use any kind of cable on stones, always get a chain around it first and hook your cable into that. Looping a cable around anything and hooking it back to itself is a good way to break it.

Figure 3-4. A wheelbarrow should have much of its load back off the wheel for maneuverability.

Figure 3-5. A-frame boom on my Land Rover being used to load heavy stone for a foundation job in Virginia. A guy cable holds the pivoting boom and another cable from the vehicle's winch goes up through a sheave and down to lift the stones.

Figure 3-6. This hydraulic bucket will lift a ton, and is very handy to get big stones into place.

HAND TOOLS

Once at the building site, you'll need the basic mason's tools for some shaping of the stone. I use a Spartan set, since I keep shaping and cutting to a minimum for a natural appearance. A heavy stone hammer, small mason's hammer, striking hammer, point, stone chisel, and pitching tool will do nicely for most jobs, although there are many more.

The heavy stone hammer (Fig. 3-7a) has a blunt edge that's used for breaking stones. The edge will direct the crack, while the mass of the hammer cracks the stone on the opposite side. This tool makes a rough break, which can be chipped smooth with the small mason's hammer.

The small mason's hammer (Fig. 3-7b) has a long blade and looks a bit like a small, narrow mattock. With the sharp edge at the end of

Figure 3-7. Stoneworking tools include (a) the stone hammer, for shaping heavy stones; (b) the mason's hammer, for light shaping; (c) the chisel, for closer controlled shaping and cutting; (d) the point, for finish work; (e) the pitching tool, for shearing to a flat surface or flaking near the edges of stones; (f) the striking hammer, for striking the chisel, point, and pitching tool. This partial set is enough for working fieldstone.

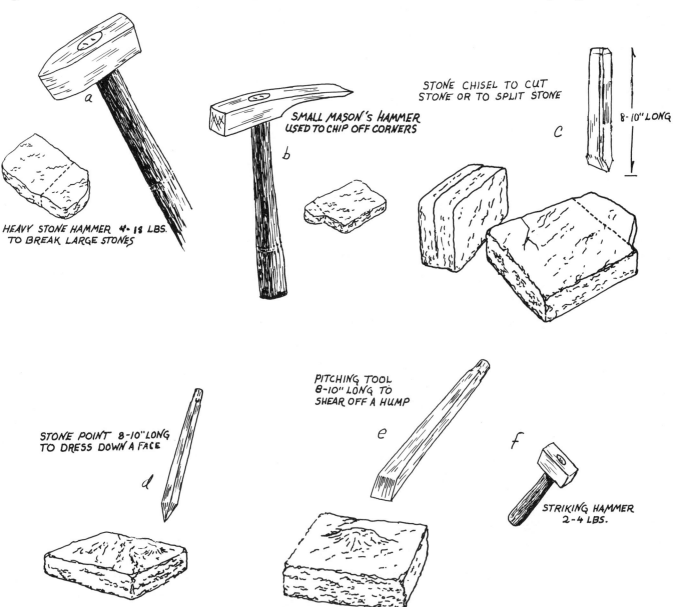

HEAVY STONE HAMMER 4-18 LBS. TO BREAK LARGE STONES

SMALL MASON'S HAMMER USED TO CHIP OFF CORNERS

STONE CHISEL TO CUT STONE OR TO SPLIT STONE

8-10" LONG

STONE POINT 8-10" LONG TO DRESS DOWN A FACE

PITCHING TOOL 8-10" LONG TO SHEAR OFF A HUMP

STRIKING HAMMER 2-4 LBS.

the blade you chip or cut, as if you had a chisel on a handle. Even big stones can be cut with this hammer if you score the surface and then go back over it repeatedly, cutting deeper each time. The hammer is best suited for shaping stones from the edges; the chisel point strikes near the edge to flake off chips.

The stone chisel, point, and pitching tools (Fig. 3-7c, d, e) are struck with the striking hammer, a flat-faced hammer of 2 to 4 pounds. The chisel is used for scoring, cutting, or chipping, but it allows more accuracy than the mason's hammer. It's good for splitting stone along the grain, too.

The point is for finish shaping, chipping away small bits, allowing close control. It's used a lot by sculptors. The pitching tool is flat on one side with a bevel on the other, allowing you to shear humps and extrusions.

These tools that are struck with a hammer (Fig. 3-7f) are used by placing the cutting edge to the stone, striking, lifting to examine and reposition, then placing again. A rhythmic tap, strike—tap, strike is the pattern.

My tools are of my own forging, of tool steel, but you probably won't find a blacksmith handy to make you a set. Beware the super-hard factory tool, though, and always wear safety glasses when cutting stone. I once used a factory-made pitching tool to take off an awkward hump from a fireplace lintel stone, the one blemish in an otherwise perfect 400-pound specimen of dense sandstone. A blow off-center sent a fragment from the brittle struck end off through my heavy trousers to tunnel deep into the muscles of my leg just above the knee. It was hard as glass and could have shattered a finger.

The end of any tool that is to be struck with a hammer should be softened, or annealed. Try a file across this end of your chisel, point, and pitching tool to test for hardness (Fig. 3-8). If the file won't cut into the steel, it needs softening. Grind a shiny spot at the end, then heat just this end till you see a blue color, then cool slowly. You can do it over a gas cookstove flame or propane torch, or in your fireplace. Don't let the color run beyond an inch or so of the struck end or you'll soften the working end, too. This isn't the method your expert toolmaker would use—and it isn't mine either—but it's one you can do easily, and it will work. You'll eventually get some mushrooming from the softened steel, but you can grind this off.

Lay stone to be worked on a bed of something soft to absorb the shock of hammering (Fig. 3-9). Several layers of old carpet on a heavy worktable do nicely. One mason I know uses wood shavings on a table with low sides to hold them in. Sawdust is good, too. You want the stone to cut, split, or be shaped where you're working on it, not across the part you want to keep intact. And you'll soon find that working a stone on rocky, uneven ground will be a lot like working or shaping glass—the cracks will go everywhere.

You may want to use the stone just as you find it, but that'll mean a lot of searching and rejecting. Minimal shaping can save a lot of time. You'll find you use the small mason's hammer most.

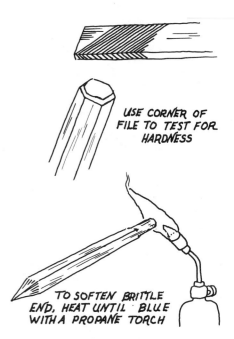

USE CORNER OF FILE TO TEST FOR HARDNESS

TO SOFTEN BRITTLE END, HEAT UNTIL BLUE WITH A PROPANE TORCH

Figure 3-8. This is a simple method of drawing the temper from the struck end of a stone tool. If left hard, there is danger of chipping off sharp bits of steel.

WORKTABLE WITH SAWDUST OR WOOD SHAVINGS TO CUSHION STONE BEING CUT

Figure 3-9. A stone-dressing table, which can be covered with sawdust, shavings, or old carpet to cushion the stone while it is shaped.

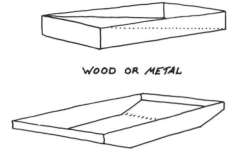

MIXING BOXES

WOOD OR METAL

Figure 3-10. Mixing boxes, sloped to make mixing easier and to keep the mortar in one place.

MORTAR TOOLS

For mixing mortar you need a hoe, shovel, and mixing box or wheelbarrow. If you're picky about measuring things, add a bucket, so you can keep the one for cement and lime dry.

A cement mixer is practical only if you have a big project going, with maybe two helpers. Working by yourself, you won't even be able to use up a modest wheelbarrowful of mortar without wetting and remixing once or twice as it dries. A mixer is good for repeated batches, so that last bit of mortar you never seem able to get out won't go to waste. With just one batch at a time, you need to wash out the mixer, and you'll waste a lot. Mixing concrete for a footing is quite another matter: a mixer is almost a necessity for that much work.

Mixing mortar in a box or wheelbarrow is hard work, but no harder than the rest of the stonework. It's a good way to warm up for the task each session. The mixing box can be wood or metal and should have a bottom sloping toward one or both ends (Fig. 3-10). This lets you get the mixing hoe in at a better angle and also makes it easier to keep the mortar all in one place as you use it, so it won't dry out as quickly.

I've stopped using a mixing box, since a large wheelbarrow holds about the right amount—2 cubic feet or so. This way I can move the mix to another part of the wall as I work. Since I don't lay more than maybe a three-vertical-stone layer at a session, I work along the wall, and the wheelbarrow is handy. Also, I load up sand at the sand pile, and cement and lime wherever they happen to be, then trundle to the work area to mix.

Let me warn of hazards here. Level ground is one thing for a wheelbarrow, a steep slope is another. One summer my neighbor, G. K. Land, and I were racing to get the concrete footing for the stone foundation of his house poured, with the help of a cement mixer. In spite of the July sun, we were going at it full tilt by loading the mixer, plunging sizzling head and shoulders into the creek below, dumping the mortar into the wheelbarrow, wheeling it to the work area, plunging into the creek, pouring a section of footing, and plunging into the creek again.

Now, this house site was and is picturesque, on a ledge above the creek. We were building a high wall up from a lower ledge on the creek side to fill against. That meant wheeling mix down a steep path to the footing area, which we usually did as a team, one of us holding the load back.

Well, I guess it was the heat; the last bit of shade had vanished just as we got started. Anyway, I broke the pattern by dumping the concrete mix, sloshing water into the mixer, then starting off with the load by myself. Even stiff mix is liquid, so we always backed down to keep it level. This particular batch seemed soupier and heavier; I don't measure things very closely, so it probably was. Anyway, it started gaining speed as I backpedaled down the twisting path—till I tripped on the inevitable root or rock and went over backwards into some dense, thorny bushes on the edge of the bank over the creek.

Fortunately, the bushes stopped me. I stopped the wheelbarrow, arms extended upward, still holding it upright and level. But the 200 pounds of cement went all over me and the landscape in general.

The worst part was my mouth was full and I couldn't express my injured feelings adequately. G.K. couldn't help laughing. He said later he'd considered just leaving me there as a statue, maybe a modern birdbath, but about then I became partially vocal again, so he changed his mind.

For laying the stones, you need a good mason's trowel—not the cheap kind put together with two weak rivets, but a good, one-piece trowel of tough steel that can let you chop a rock in two (Fig. 3-11). These usually come with a sharp point, which you can grind to about a half-inch round tip. The point will get in your way on rock worth.

Get a second, smaller trowel for close work. You may want to use this one a lot till you get the hang of the bigger one. If I can get the wheelbarrow close to my work, I just trowel mortar onto the stones. If not, I use the shovel or a flat board to transport it.

Wire-brush everything after you're through working. Once mortar dries on your tools the next layers build up, and it's very hard to get off. A cement mixer is easy to clean with just water and maybe a little gravel as it turns, but improperly cleaned it builds up solid concrete inside. And don't get mortar on your hands. It takes the skin off unless you wash it off quickly. Resist the temptation to push mortar into cracks with your fingers; with practice you can do it better with the trowel anyway.

Have some plastic sheeting to cover fresh stonework to keep it moist. And use the wire brush to recess the mortar joints and clean up smeared mortar after it has dried to a crumbly state. Use gloves here; the stone will skin every knuckle you have.

You'll also need a level, square, plumb bob, tape measure, and string to keep things straight.

Compared to building with other materials, the tools necessary for stonework are few. You're dealing with a very natural, permanent material, and the less you change it, the better.

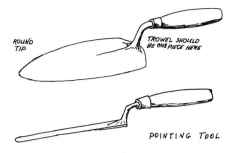

Figure 3-11. A good trowel should be one piece and of tough steel. A mixing hoe has holes in it, but a sturdy garden hoe will do for mortar work.

You will also need a good pointing tool, which is a narrow trowel-like blade, 3/8" to 3/4" wide. You use this to push the mortar into cracks between the stones after you've laid them.

Figure 3-12. Use the pointing tool to push mortar off the trowel and into spaces between stones set in place.

Figure 4-1. The Jolly Mill in Newton County, Missouri, has a drystone foundation of nicely worked sandstone blocks, some eight feet long.

DRYSTONE WORK

LAYING UP STONE DRY is the best way to learn to handle this material. It gives you the basics for any kind of refined stonework you might get into later.

I've found that one basic rule will keep you out of trouble with stonework better than any other: Each stone should be laid so that it will stay in place dry, whether you intend to mortar it or not. That reduces the function of the mortar as a bond and lets you put up a hell of a wall. More on mortar later.

Drystone was used by the early builders in foundations, as flagstone in floors and roads, to line root cellars, wells, and cisterns, to hold eroding soil, to strengthen dams, and it is still used in walls and fences. In rocky country you have to stack the stones *somewhere*.

They key to drystone work is fitting the rocks—fitting them well, not so they just barely stand. You see, a drystone wall is always in motion, as the moist ground freezing underneath bulges upward and as slanting sunlight warms and expands one side of each stone. These rocks must be laid so that they can flex a bit and not fall.

Some will inevitably fall, with the added pressures of small trees growing among the cracks, children scrambling over, and large animals rubbing against them. But mending a wall is a pleasant task—if we are to believe Robert Frost—and an ongoing one.

TECHNIQUE

Let's start with a wall that doesn't do anything like hold back a mountain or the urban hordes. Call it a stone fence, which might be your property boundary or simply the border of a field of your yard. First, clear the surface debris from along the route of the wall. I like to scuff away the sod, too, and cut any surface tree roots, giving me a better ground to start with. Remember that you cannot eliminate the ground's heaving with frost unless you go below the frost line and seal out moisture, but you can at least make a good, solid start.

Lay as much stone as possible in ledge pattern—that means use flat stones laid horizontally if you have them. If you don't have flat stones, select those that have more or less flat top and bottom, however thick they may be. If your stones look like bowling balls, don't try drystone work with them. Use your stone tools to shape crucial flat places, and watch for flying rock chips. You can also break them into chunks with a sledge, and some of the pieces will be usable.

Lay your wall thick enough so that you can use at least two stones to get from inside to outside, sloping them inward. Bind with a single tie stone whenever you find one large enough. It's the same principle as laying a brick wall that's two bricks thick, turning some bricks to span the thickness, as in English or Flemish bond.

With drystone you tilt the stones inward so their weight pushes against one another and helps return them to position as they flex (Fig. 4-6). That assumes you have some stones that are thicker at one edge than another, and many will be. I never tire of the game of fitting stones, none of which are even similar. Bricks, now, and concrete blocks, have that moronic sameness that makes them better building materials but endears them to no creative person.

Cover each vertical crack with the next stone up (Figs. 4-7, 4-8). If you place a thick rock next to a thin one because they fit so well, you won't be able to span the crack. Try to find another thin one to bring it to near level, or lay another thin one on top of the thick one, and another thick one on the thin one. That gives you two thicknesses up with a common vertical crack. Don't go any more than two.

VERTICAL RUNNING JOINTS

If you study any stone wall—dry or mortared—with a vertical fracture in it, you'll find that it has taken a path through the weaker verticals left by the mason and broken only those stones that directly blocked its path. If during construction you have a vertical crack that unavoidably extends upward with only minor weavings around the ends of stones, block it squarely with a huge rock and get it stopped.

Not one of these stones is going to fit neatly atop another. They will all totter and crunch and rock back and forth. Wedge them with bits of broken rock or gravel where you cannot achieve a fit, but don't make these wedges carry much of the weight. Let's say the 50-pound stone you just laid rocks a half inch on two diagonally opposite corners. Let's say also that it's one that reaches halfway through

Figure 4-2. A drystone chimney still standing after the cabin fell. Cracks have been plastered where drafts would affect the fire inside. This chimney is near the Blue Ridge in Virginia.

Figure 4-3. This drystone wall in Newton County, Missouri, sheltered Confederate soldiers during a skirmish. Stones are the ledge sandstone of the area.

your wall. Rocking it down at the outside lets it sit solidly on three points, with one inside corner up. Wedge it this way, since you'll have it tilted inward anyway, with the weight from above on the outside, or high, edge. If you rock it inward and edge the outside, that weight will probably crush the wedge or work it out in time and loosen the stone (Fig. 4-9).

I suppose you'd have to say there's some physics involved in dry-stone work, but it's more like plain common sense. If you take time to figure out what has to happen to make a particular rock do what it's supposed to, you can find a way to make it happen. When you wedge any stone in a wall, do it solidly, since the whole structure above it will be thrown off if the wedge crushes or falls out.

Figure 4-4. This Stone County, Arkansas, wall is of the excellent ledge sandstone of the area. Six feet tall in places, it winds around and over hills reminiscent of Scotland and Wales.

Figure 4-5. I train masons by having them do drystone walls first. This is a retaining wall of leftover stone from Greystone, a house we built in central Virginia, which was carpenter Noah Bradley's first-time stone effort.

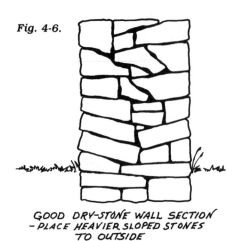

Fig. 4-6.

GOOD DRY-STONE WALL SECTION
– PLACE HEAVIER SLOPED STONES
TO OUTSIDE

Figure 4-6. Stones in a dry wall should be tilted inward, with small pieces filling in the center. A drystone structure is always in motion from temperature changes.

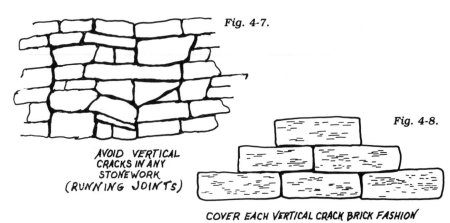

Fig. 4-7.

AVOID VERTICAL
CRACKS IN ANY
STONEWORK
(RUNNING JOINTS)

Fig. 4-8.

COVER EACH VERTICAL CRACK BRICK FASHION

Figures 4-7 and 4-8. Avoid vertical cracks like this when laying dry or mortared stone. Stone should be laid brick or shingle fashion, with each stone covering the crack beneath it.

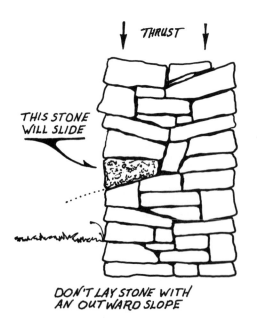

THRUST

THIS STONE
WILL SLIDE

DON'T LAY STONE WITH
AN OUTWARD SLOPE

Figure 4-9. Each stone in a wall should be laid so that it stays in place by itself, whether it is to be mortared or not. The outward slope of the one stone shown here would let it slide out of a dry wall or weaken a mortared wall.

You'll spend a lot of time looking for the right rock. If one won't fit, put two in, break a corner off, wedge, and fill with small stones at the center of the wall. The idea is always to give a good surface to the next stone above to fit onto.

I don't advise using dirt or clay to fill spaces in a stone wall; rain will wash it out. This used to be common, and it is still acceptable practice in a drystone foundation that will stay dry, but you can't really predict how much dirt will compress under weight.

We haven't talked about the dimensions of your dry wall, other than that it should be at least two rocks thick. I like a thickness of 2 feet for a wall 3 feet high, continuing that 2-to-3 proportion as you go higher. If you build a 6-foot wall 4 feet thick, you'll have trouble finding and handling tie stones 4 feet long. So you tie from each side, as far across as your stones will reach, alternating.

If your wall goes downhill, scoop out the ground in steps so that you start level, then try to stay level. A sloping joint or crack will always mean the rock above it will creep down along it. If you've laid a rock that leaves you with a sloping top surface, it doesn't help to correct it with a thick-edged rock above it. The slope is still there. You can correct it if you have a reverse slope next to it so the two stones can slide against each other. All the thrusts and pressures inside the wall come directly from the pull of gravity, working with or against temperature force changes, so a bit of study will tell you how this force will affect the stone shapes.

As time goes by, the weight of your wall will work with the flexing of natural forces to shift stress points, and the wall will become more stable if it's laid right. If not, it'll start falling apart. For example, if you've left a corner of one rock 1/8 inch up off the one under it, the weight from above might break the stone, letting the pieces down— or over the years, that weight concentrated on the other corners will drive them down until the gap closes, making it more solid.

With your wall up to height, you can cap it in any of several ways.

Flat stones, if they're thin, tend to get pushed off. Flat stones standing on edge and wedged in tightly last longer and have been popular in the past (Fig 4-11).

I like to cap with thick, flat stones laid ledge (flat), to keep out as much water as possible (Fig. 4-10). Over a long winter, a lot of freezing moisture can concentrate down in the wall and push it apart. The less rain, sleet, and snow you let get in there, the better.

With chunks or rounded stones, there's not much you can do to shelter the wall from the top. Sloping top surfaces outward will help somewhat, and this means using thick-edged, sloping stones. Again, use larger stones here if you can get them up that high. Their weight helps keep them in place, and there is more area per stone to shed water between cracks.

These cracks will invite every kind of inhabitant. Drystone is natural and attractive, and you should do some of it before you go on to other types of stonework, but be aware of the haven you are creating for snakes, spiders, wasps, scorpions, field mice, lizards, and even birds. Good and bad. If you're one who enjoys sharing your homestead with wild creatures, a drystone wall is for you. If you're not, go for a redwood fence or something like that.

Figure 4-10. These cemetery wall capstones were shaped to a crown in an unusual treatment.

VERTICAL CAPSTONES

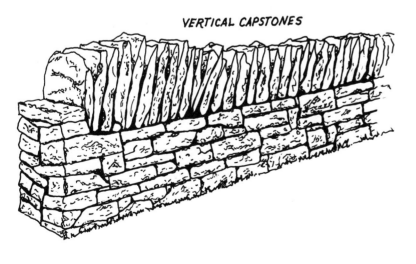

Figure 4-11. Rural drystone walls were often capped with a vertical course, probably to discourage climbing. I prefer heavy stones laid flat.

Figure 4-12. Although not a drystone
mass, this mortared "dry look" retaining
wall is sloped against the bank to help hold
it.

RETAINING WALLS

A stone retaining wall will keep a hill or bank of fill dirt where it belongs if it's well built (Fig. 4-12). I have seen lots of them poorly built, which usually adds the stones themselves to the tons of dirt that tumble down across the builder's daisies.

Let's assume you've either cut into a hillside or filled an area and want to hold the cut or fill with a drystone wall. Remember that the soil will try to push your wall over, so you must build the wall to push back. It seems logical to lean the wall, which is fine if you want to look at a leaning wall—you could plant things in it and make it charming— but you'd limit the level ground you're holding in place at the top (Fig. 4-15).

I start with a thin wall, say 6 inches at the base. Then I widen or thicken it, filling in and packing the dirt as I go up (Fig. 4-13). Put down a layer of stone, then pull fill dirt up to it, level with the top. To get rid of air pockets, pack it with the end of a prybar or something pointed, or water it down. Keep filling so the dirt is even with the top of the rock.

Now lay the next layer of wider stones that extend back over some of the fill, keeping the outside face of the wall vertical. More fill, packing, another layer of yet wider stones. Use two or more at the top to get, say, 2 feet of wall thickness at a 3-foot height.

The fill or cutbank will tend to push more at the top where your wall leans into it most (Fig. 4-14). The packed dirt at the bottom is being compressed by all that weight, as are the smaller stones, so both dirt and stones stay put.

When you're filling against a slope, you can minimize outward thrust by cutting steps into the hill (Figs. 4-16, 4-17). That way the loose fill will bear directly down and not tend to push outward so much.

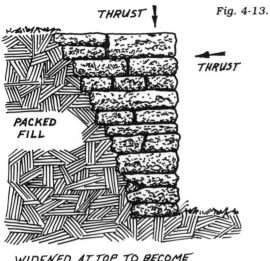

THRUST

Fig. 4-13.

THRUST

PACKED
FILL

WIDENED AT TOP TO BECOME
PART OF HILL

Figure 4-13. This retaining wall lets you have a vertical face and saves usable level space.

Fig. 4-14.

SOLID
CUT
BANK

Figure 4-14. Against a firm-cut bank, build the retaining wall leading into the mass and fill against it at the bottom. The firm cut will loosen in time and push outward more.

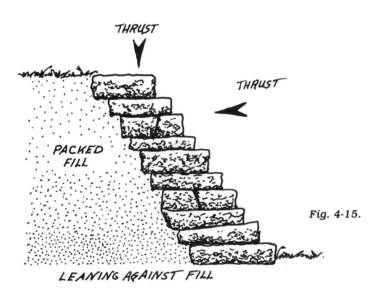

THRUST

THRUST

PACKED
FILL

Fig. 4-15.

LEANING AGAINST FILL

Figure 4-15. One way to hold a slope with drystone as a retaining wall. The outward push of the earth is balanced by the inward push of the off-center stones.

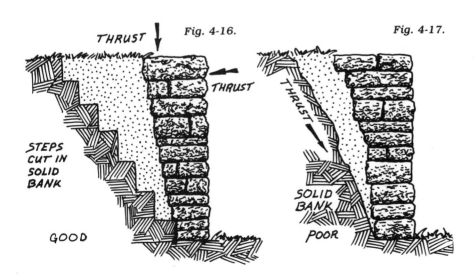

THRUST

Fig. 4-16.

THRUST

STEPS
CUT IN
SOLID
BANK

GOOD

Fig. 4-17.

THRUST

SOLID
BANK

POOR

Figures 4-16 and 4-17. Fill dirt on a slope tends to push outward harder and require a stronger retaining wall. When the slope is stepped, much of the push is downward, and a lighter wall will hold.

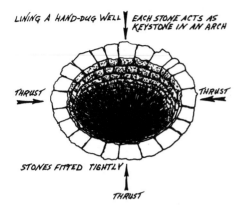

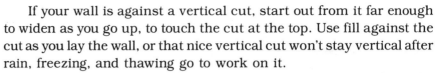

Figure 4-18. Lining a hand-dug well involves circular courses of drystone laid as in an arch, with each wedged to hold the soil from caving in.

If your wall is against a vertical cut, start out from it far enough to widen as you go up, to touch the cut at the top. Use fill against the cut as you lay the wall, or that nice vertical cut won't stay vertical after rain, freezing, and thawing go to work on it.

Don't give in to the temptation to build a straight wall against fill or a cut. With time, even the packed subsoil of the cut will shift outward, and you'll have only the weight of the stones to hold it. And a straight wall, even a mortared one, won't hold against loose fill trying to seek a level, aided by the thrusts of freezing moisture.

A retaining wall is essentially a dam, holding back earth in an unnatural situation. You have only the force of gravity working for you, and that's also what you're working against. Both a dam and a retaining wall can be strengthened by using buttresses or by curving them in toward the impounded earth or water. We'll talk more about this in Chapter Fifteen, on dams.

WELLS AND CELLARS

Lining a hand-dug well or a root cellar involves the same principles as the retaining wall and dam. A root cellar is usually dug into a hillside, then lined with stone to keep it from caving in, just like a wall to hold a three-dimensional cutbank, with a top. The thing to remember is to keep the cut from moving in on your apples or potatoes or canned goods, just as you kept the hillside off your flower beds with the retaining wall. We'll have a whole chapter on this useful structure later.

It is essential to line a hand-dug well or the well will cave in under the accelerated erosion of water coming into it from all sides. Since the well should be a cylinder, the principle is different. You're using an elongated, continuous horizontal arch to keep the soil back (Fig. 4-18). Properly laid, it will be there forever.

You see, the soil pushes inward from all directions against your circle of stones, wedging them against each other tighter all the time. We'll talk about the arch and how it works later. For now you should remember to lay a ledge pattern (one with horizontal layers) of tapered stones placed so they cannot push inward and get past each other. This means more careful fitting, but it is nothing more than a continuous wall, like the one your scorpions are living in down in the meadow. It is dry-wall, of course, to let the water through.

The chances of your actually digging a well and lining it are remote, although I've dug several myself. The sad fact is that the water you'd get in your well today would most likely be too polluted to use. For irrigation or non-household use, a good case might be made for digging your own well, but the flow is usually insufficient. And digging a well is probably the hardest work I know.

If you do it, lay the lining right up out of the ground to form the well box, which I'd suggest you mortar since it'll get bumped a lot (Fig. 4-19). A beautiful old practice was to quarry a slab of stone for the top,

Figure 4-19. Finish the well with mortared stone aboveground for strength, and pave the area with flagstone to keep down mud. The stone here is especially picturesque.

Figure 4-20. Ledge sandstone well-box lid with a hole cut for the bucket. Well chain or rope wore the grooves around the edges.

Figure 4-21. Quarried limestone trough at Bethel, Missouri, from the original settlement by a religious colony. The stone is finished with the stone point, a tool for close work. I have not been able to determine the function of the stone wheels at the left of the picture.

Figure 4-22. Stone lye trough also at Bethel Colony, Missouri. The wooden ash hopper was supported by uprights set into the square holes at the corners. Lye for soap-making ran out the spout.

Figure 4-23. Slabs of sandstone on edge are mortared and plastered to form this well box near Parthenon, Arkansas. A stone with a round hole for the bucket covers the box.

with a round hole cut in it for the bucket (Fig. 4-20). The hole was covered with a smaller slab or a wooden cover.

Lay flagstone around the well box so it won't be a sea of mud from splashed water (Fig. 4-19). I've seen water troughs set nearby, hewn from solid blocks of stone, as an ambitious but craftsmanlike addition. That would take a while. We used one of concrete on the farm of my childhood.

FOUNDATIONS

Drystone foundations have been around for thousands of years. Getting the building up off the damp ground has always been important, to discourage termites and rot. And with the use of a heavy sill to distribute the weight of the structure, stone laid dry is still quite useful.

It's not essential to dig below frost line for drystone, because moisture gets into the work and freezes anyway. It *is* important to dig a wide trench, deep enough to distribute the weight over a large area to resist settling. My rule is to make a base twice the thickness of the foundation wall, which should in turn be twice the thickness of the building wall that will be on it (Fig. 4-24).

So a 6-inch building wall should go onto a 12-inch stone foundation set on a dry footing base 24 inches wide. This should be deep enough to get down below soft topsoil. In situations where the topsoil is very deep, go down enough to increase downward friction and to get the weight you're concentrating more nearly relative to the weight of the dirt you're displacing.

That's always been a complicated concept for me. It's simpler and easier just to dig below frost line in your area, just as you would for a poured footing (which we'll talk about more in Chapter Five). A drystone foundation is usually considered in order to save time and effort, so an elaborate trench and belowground work sort of defeat the purpose.

A foundation for a house is like one for a fireplace chimney. You're putting tremendous weight on a small area, so spread it around. While it doesn't matter much if your stone wall settles a couple of inches, settling can do ugly things to your house, because it rarely occurs evenly all around.

To lay your foundation wall, use the same principles as for your basic stone wall, but for stability keep it to a thickness of one stone. The weight of a sill can push a double-wall foundation apart in time. Ideally, you could do as was done a lot in New England with quarried granite: Set a single long slab up on edge and be done with a whole section at a time. There's really no point in setting bolts to anchor the sills—or any practical way to do so—since each stone in the foundation is loose. You're counting on gravity to hold it all in place anyway.

At the corners, alternate long stones, again laid in a ledge pattern if possible, to bind the work together (Fig. 4-25). If you don't have a smooth surface for your sills, you can drive pieces of stone in later to take the weight better. For a hewn-log house foundation, I usually use stone only at the corners, with one narrow stone supporting pier halfway down each wall. The logs, often 12 to 16 inches high and 6 inches or more thick each, take the weight nicely with only this support. If I were laying a 2-inch sill flat, I'd insist on a continuous foundation wall, flat enough on top for almost constant contact with the wood (Fig. 4-26).

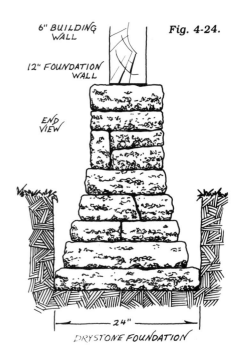

Fig. 4-24.

6" BUILDING WALL

12" FOUNDATION WALL

END VIEW

24"

DRYSTONE FOUNDATION

Figure 4-24. Use only one stone thickness under the sill, since slow flexing with temperature changes could allow the sill to settle between two stones. Also, a wide stone base distributes the weight better.

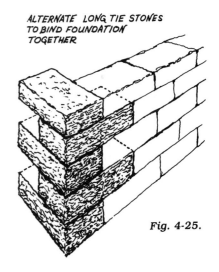

ALTERNATE LONG TIE STONES TO BIND FOUNDATION TOGETHER

Fig. 4-25.

Figure 4-25. Cornering a stone wall. A header should always overlap a stretcher at the corners for strength, in either a drystone or mortared stone wall. As a foundation, this is especially important.

Figure 4-26. Drystone makes a good foundation with a heavy sill on top. The weight is distributed by the sill so that unevenness in the stones is no great drawback.

Fig. 4-26.

SILL

SILL SHOULD COME IN CONTACT WITH DRY FOUNDATION AS MUCH AS POSSIBLE

DRYSTONE STEPS

Steps are a refining touch to garden or landscape work. Drystone is ideal, since there's so little work involved. I like to cut steps into the ground of the slope, then fit a single slab of stone for the riser and one or more, as flagstone, for the tread (Fig. 4-27).

With steps cut this way, the riser stone can be notched into firm soil at each end and the tread extended over it for a solid step. Done with loose fill, there's much more of a tendency for the earth to slide and push over the riser.

Fifteen years ago, photographer Jack Cofield and I did a series of steps up a steep slope in his garden in Oxford, Mississippi, using only the single stone riser and gravel over soil for the tread. This won't work the other way around—with stone tread and dirt riser—because rainwater will undercut the stone and collapse it. More than one stone for the riser will also let it fall. I saw those steps again last year, and they're still sound, mellowed into the garden wonderfully.

If you use several stones for the tread, there's no point in mortaring the joints because they'll crack apart anyway. Let the grass

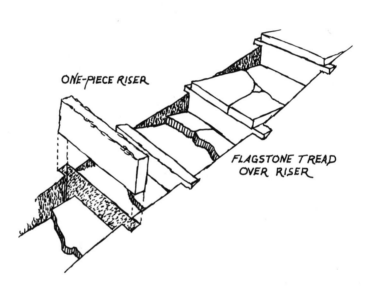

ONE-PIECE RISER

FLAGSTONE TREAD OVER RISER

Figure 4-27. Stone steps can be laid of thin stone by setting each riser into firm soil. Then one or more pieces of flagstone—or gravel or soil—can be the tread.

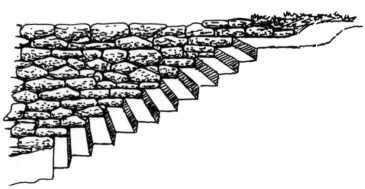

BUILD AT AN ANGLE UP A STEEP SLOPE TO KEEP STEPS TO A 7×12" MAXIMUM. USE A RETAINING WALL TO HOLD THE CUT YOU MAKE.

Figure 4-28. Steps can traverse a slope to minimize steepness, with a retaining wall to hold the cut bank. A 7-inch riser and a 12-inch tread make a good flight of steps.

grow up between them; you won't be able to keep it out.

Steps should be proportioned to allow comfortable use. Anything less than a 12-inch tread is awkward, and even dangerous on a steep slope. And 7 inches for the riser is a reasonable maximum (Fig. 4-28). If your slope is steeper, you can go across it with combination steps and a retaining wall and achieve a nice effect.

If the slope is more gradual, group the steps and alternate with flagstone paving. Don't lay a very deep tread that requires two or more steps to get across it. Folks expect an evenness to steps and will stumble if you vary it without pattern.

A SPECIAL CRAFT

Drystone work has its obvious advantages and its limitations. You need better stone for drystone work than for mortared work, both for strength and for fitting. Ledge stone is best for any type of dry work, and New England rounded granite is a real challenge. So are limerock-country chert and flint nodules. Broken or blasted stone can be used, but it means a lot of picking and choosing because there's no pattern to the jagged shapes.

Most important, building with drystone gives you an understanding of the material and a knowledge of its limitations that will make your mortared work stronger and better looking.

And you'll begin to think more like a Stone Age type, a back-to-basics change from your nine-to-five programming.

Figure 4-29. Limestone steps and retaining wall, G.K. Land house, combining creek stones with cut stone from old foundations.

Figure 5-1. Part of the combined foundation and millrace at Turnback Mill in Lawrence County, Missouri. This work, not visible in the finished restoration, is for strength, with heavy mortar joints not raked or struck.

MORTARED STONE

MORTAR IS THE BONDING, filling substance that binds the stone in a structure together in one mass. Because it is at first a stiff semi-liquid, it can conform to all the irregular spaces between stones, distributing weight and stress evenly. Then it hardens, to function much as the stone itself.

Mortar keeps out water so that it doesn't get between the rocks, freeze, and push them apart. It keeps out seedlings and roots that will crack a wall as they grow. It strengthens the stone structure, adding its binding effect to the inertia of gravity that holds drystone work.

MUD—NOT GLUE

One thing you should understand about mortar, or "mud," as it's commonly called among masons (and beginners hasten to drop the term at every opportunity): It is not an all-purpose glue to stick misshapen rocks into odd spaces. The stones should first fit, as you learned in Chapter Four. Reflect on the fact that for centuries stone was often laid quite successfully with clay or real mud as mortar and that the lime-and-sand that followed was a crumbly, soft substance that bonded just a little better than clay.

The old brick and stone walls you see with the mortar joints eroded deeply where the weather has touched them are usually lime mortar. The secret was to keep these soft mortars out of the rain, under roofs or eaves.

You may use clay or lime-and-sand today, but there's really not much point to it. The masonry cement we build with now is weatherproof enough for foreseeable generations, holds well, and is not outrageously expensive. I recall Thoreau's comment on the high price of lime while building his hut at Walden Pond.

Masonry cement is different from the portland or standard cement used in concrete. Concrete is an aggregate of cement, sand, and gravel. It is hard and strong, especially when reinforced with steel, making it a good building material in itself. Masonry mortar is a filler, similar to plaster, that bonds stones together.

I know rural masons who use portland cement for laying stone because it sets harder and, they reason, makes a better wall. The trouble is it has virtually no flexibility, so its shrinkage as it dries usually cracks it. But masonry mortar will give a bit under stress, though not

Lime in mortar also holds moisture, allowing slower and better curing.

as much as lime or clay, and it resists cracking. With the constant expansion and contraction of a stone structure with temperature changes, this flexibility is necessary.

You may buy masonry cement at your local building supply house or lumber company. What you'll get is essentially a mix of portland cement and lime, giving you the strength of the one and the flexibility of the other.

MIX PROPORTIONS

Or you can buy sacks of portland and of lime and mix them, which is what I do because it's cheaper. There are mixing formulas in several of the handbooks on masonry, such as Audell's, and they usually center around a half-and-half mix. I've gone to a mix of 1 lime to 2 portland with a resulting stronger bond, still without cracking. Also, my mix is a shade darker in color.

Mix your ready-made masonry cement or your own mix with sand in one of the accepted proportions. I find that local masons in different parts of the country favor richer or leaner mixes, apparently because of weather extremes and the characteristics of their stones. I use a mix of 1 part masonry cement to 3 parts sand as a standard.

If the sand is river sand, which has rounded corners from wear, I use a richer mix, say 1 to 2½. A sharp sand, like that washed from sandy soil or deposited from erosion along a roadside ditch, sticks together with less cement, and I have used it 1 to 4. Once I chanced on a pile of clean sand in a junkyard, of all places. Not one to miss a bet, I scooped up some of it for some stonework I was doing at the time. Well, the stuff wouldn't stick together unless I laced it with cement, about a 1-to-1 proportion. I wondered about that. It was evident that the sand was rounded, but I'd never seen river sand that loose. I'd thought the sand came from a water filter unit, which often uses sand and charcoal, but I was wrong. It had come from a sand-blaster and was just plain worn round.

My standard mix is actually, then, 1 part lime to 2 parts portland to 9 parts sand—or ⅓ to ⅔ to 3 (Fig. 5-2). Mix this thoroughly with a shovel or hoe in a large wheelbarrow or mixing box, for a uniform dry mix. Now add water, mixing with the hoe as you do. This is a more or less crucial stage of your work, because the consistency of the mortar is quite important. It should definitely stand in peaks like whipped cream—too thin, it runs all over everything; too stiff, it's hard

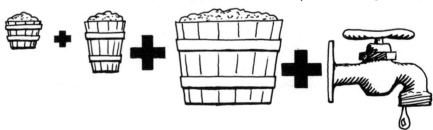

⅓ PART LIME + ⅔ PARTS CEMENT + 3 PARTS SAND + ENOUGH WATER FOR A STIFF MIX

Figure 5-2. This is the basic mortar formula I use. With pit sand, which is sharper, I use less lime and cement; with river (rounded) sand I use more.

to mix and doesn't bond well. Most masons go for a stiff mix, which is neater, but you can usually see back into spaces in their work that just didn't flow together.

Stop adding water before you think it's time, because the last cupful usually gets the mortar too thin. Somehow it seems to go from quite dry to quite soupy with just a dash more. If it's really too dry, do add a bit more water. You'll have to as it dries while you're working anyway. If it's too runny, you have three choices: (1) add cement and sand; (2) go away for a half hour, during which time much of the excess water rises to the top and can be carefully poured off; or (3) wait a few minutes for the water to start rising, then dig clear to the bottom of your mixing box and get trowelfuls of comparatively stiff mortar (that the water has floated up from) to start with. It'll still be loose, but you can also pile some up on the dry stone of your wall and let some of the water be absorbed and evaporate faster.

Don't lay stone with gooey mortar. It's hard to get all of it off after it runs and drips, and as it flows down and out it leaves hollows that weaken your work. Minute air pockets that form as the water dries will weaken it too.

A dry mortar mix, while easier to clean up, will allow rain water to leak through chimneys or outside walls.

FINISHING MORTAR WORK

After mortar is applied, there are two important things you must do to it. The first is structural, the second is cosmetic. Dry cement is not necessarily cured cement. Mortar and concrete should both be cured—kept moist for up to six days—for the chemical action to be complete. Letting it dry out stops the bonding process, and you'll have little more than sand in your wall. Cover it with plastic sheeting or wet burlap bags, wetting a couple of times a day after it's too hard to run or wash out.

One July, I hired an enthusiastic young giant, whom I knew had experience with masonry work, to help with a hewn-log house. He laid the stone foundation beautifully, with the joints struck deeply, lichens preserved: fine wall. But he didn't keep his work moist. I was off on the logging expeditions for the job and didn't suspect a thing until we set the 800-pound sill log. His stonework collapsed under just that weight. Seems all the work he'd done before had been ornamental stone in landscape situations, where there was no stress involved.

The other thing to remember is to uncover the stonework four to twelve hours after it's laid and strike the joints, that is, recess the mortar between the stones. This can be done to a degree with very dry mortar as you work, but it always looks better if you go over it again with a wire brush after it's crumbly (Fig. 5-4). Then cover it again. Spray water on it periodically, after it's too hard to wash out, until the mortar has cured.

Any smears are also best brushed off at this crumbly stage. Really stubborn ones can be removed with a weak solution of 1 part muriatic acid to 10 parts water. Of course, any lichens or moss will

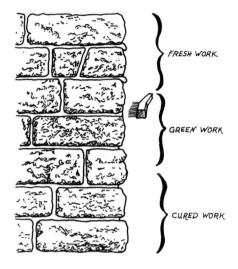

Figure 5-3. Lay only two or three courses a day to allow the mortar to cure partially before going higher. "Green" mortar is semi-cured but fairly firm and can be wire-brushed for uniformly struck joints. Fresh work should stand overnight before being cleaned up. The wall should be dampened and covered with plastic for several days to prevent the mortar from drying before it's cured.

be killed by smeared mortar, brushing, or the acid. You'd have to keep these growths consistently moist to keep them alive anyway.

It isn't necessary to cure each section of wall completely before you add more stone. By the second day the mortar will be more or less rigid, or "green," and you can lay more stone on it if you are careful. If you bump a part of the wall with a large stone or drop something heavy on it, you can knock it loose at this stage.

It isn't a good idea to lay more than, say, three vertical courses a day. More would increase the probability of the new work's tipping before the mortar sets up (Fig. 5-3). I know masons who routinely lay 3 vertical feet or more on a fireplace chimney a day, which may be six courses, to go on with six more on the green work the next day, and finish the job in a week. This rushing of things will get you into trouble, and it turns a pleasant task into a headlong, odious chore. Of course, on a fireplace chimney you'll have so little horizontal wall length to lay that you'll get three courses up in less than a day, after you get the hang of laying stone. I like to spell stone-laying with gathering trips and other aspects of the total job.

On the subject of colored mortar for stonework, I have little to say. Colored mortar has always looked unnatural to me, and I never use it. The darkened mortar is supposed to make the stones stand out better, but to my eye it has never succeeded—looks like some quickie glue. Recessed joints cast a natural shadow that sets the stone off better. It looks as though it's standing out because it is, and that's the kind of honest work I like.

Figure 5-4. Wire-brushing stonework the day after laying it. Joints can be raked with a pointing tool, then wire-brushed to make the stone stand out.

STRUCK OR RAKED JOINTS LOOK BEST

You can't strike the joints on veneer work very deep, but even ¼ inch helps. On ledge pattern work, where you have plenty of depth, go 1 inch or so. The more you recess the joints, and the thinner you make the joints, the more natural and like drystone work it looks.

More lime makes the mortar lighter, since lime is essentially what whitewash is made of. My 1-to-2 lime-cement mix results in a neutral gray that is lighter than most masons want, but I like it. Old-timers sometimes mixed soot in their mortar. A little darkening may be acceptable to you, but it's soon overdone.

A mortared stone structure isn't just drystone work with mix thrown in. In his excellent book *Building Stone Walls* (Pownal, Vt.: Garden Way Publishing, 1976), John Vivian notes that the movement of the wall will crack out this simple pointing up.

THE FOOTING

A footing of reinforced concrete below the frost line will stabilize the structure, making it a solid unit so that mortared joints won't crack. The footing spreads the weight over a wider area, to resist settling, and seals out moisture in amounts that could freeze and break the work apart. See Fig. 5-5.

Dig a trench at least twice the width of the stone wall or foundation that will be built on it, to a depth below frost line in your area. This can be 6 inches in the southern United States or over 2 feet up north. In southwest Missouri, I dig 12 to 18 inches and usually hit rock ledges about there. Solid rock is fine, except that your structure rarely sits completely atop it. Just one corner on soil, even with a wide footing, and your wall will settle and eventually crack.

The deeper the footing, the more nearly the weight of your total structure approaches the weight of the soil you're displacing, so the less tendency there is to settle. Frank Lloyd Wright explained this in telling how he had concrete pilings set 8 feet deep in the spongy soil of Japan for the Imperial Hotel. Friction also increases with greater foundation depth and area, so settling is still less.

I dig a 24-inch trench for a 12-inch stone wall, then pour a minimum 6-inch-thick footing reinforced with at least two ½-inch rods. These are placed midway up the footing concrete, far enough in from the edges to support the weight of the stone directly above.

It isn't necessary to fill the trench with concrete. You want a slab heavy enough to distribute the weight without breaking, and you want to seal out water. So you can come up to ground level with stone laid tightly with mortar. Spaces here would allow ice to form above frost line, which would heave the wall, even with the footing below. See Fig. 5-8.

Figure 5-5. A mortared wall should have a footing of reinforced concrete, sealing out water to below frost line. This is to keep ice from forming under the wall and heaving it, eventually cracking and breaking it apart.

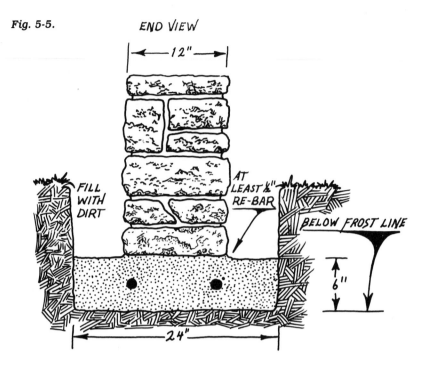

Fig. 5-5.

END VIEW

12"

FILL WITH DIRT

AT LEAST ½" RE-BAR

BELOW FROST LINE

6"

24"

Figure 5-6. When a footing must go uphill or downhill, step it with the slope, using upright boards to hold the liquid concrete. This gives a level surface to lay stone on and keeps the whole thing from sliding downhill.

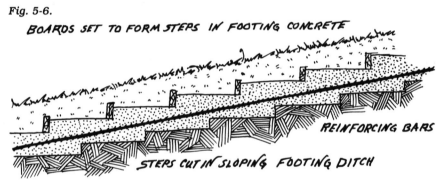

Fig. 5-6.

BOARDS SET TO FORM STEPS IN FOOTING CONCRETE

REINFORCING BARS

STEPS CUT IN SLOPING FOOTING DITCH

Figures 5-7 and 5-8. A footing in soft ground or extending onto soil from solid rock should be heavier, with more reinforcing, to avoid settling and cracking. Stone can be laid on a dry footing of crushed or broken stone, which allows water to drain away below frost line. Some building codes do not allow this, however.

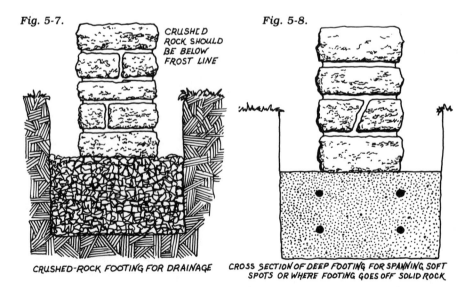

Fig. 5-7.

CRUSHED ROCK SHOULD BE BELOW FROST LINE

CRUSHED-ROCK FOOTING FOR DRAINAGE

Fig. 5-8.

CROSS SECTION OF DEEP FOOTING FOR SPANNING SOFT SPOTS OR WHERE FOOTING GOES OFF SOLID ROCK

Step the footing ditch if it goes uphill, in order to have level surfaces to work on. This will mean a thicker footing so the steps won't expose the reinforcing rods, so plan accordingly. I pour half the concrete, place the rods, then set boards or flat stones across to form the tops of the steps. See Fig. 5-6.

Modern contractors in a hurry will set the rods beforehand, often through holes in bricks up on end. This makes a "cold" joint right down to the ground that weakens the footing and can allow moisture to rust the steel rods. They should be floated in and sealed by the concrete for greatest strength.

REINFORCING

A word here about reinforcing concrete. Steel, even flexible steel like old cable or wire, becomes rigid in concrete and makes it vastly stronger. Without reinforcing, concrete has the strength of crumbly stone. With steel in it, we span rivers and gorges with concrete and hold back lakes and mountains.

I recall a handyman in northern Arkansas who built a septic tank entirely of concrete with no reinforcing, not even in the lid. He moved away soon afterward, but I often wonder when that lid will give way under the new owners.

For reinforced concrete to sag and break, the steel inside must stretch—hence its strength. The ridges on reinforcing steel help keep it from slipping under strain. If you use old cable or wire or smooth rods, you lose a bit of this holding power.

Prestressed concrete, such as that used in beams, is purposely distorted by stretching the steel before the concrete is poured into the form. The steel is located in that part of the beam where stress will be greatest in use (near the bottom for a beam to span a distance, near the top for one that is to cantilever at the ends). The stretching tension is released after the concrete is cured, bowing the beam against its eventual load.

LIKE A BEAM

A footing is basically a beam laid in the ground, conforming to the irregular shape of the subsoil, carrying a load as a beam does overhead. Since there will be heavier and lighter parts of the structure on the footing, it's hard to know where to expect maximum stress. For this reason I reinforce at the center. If I were to build a very high, heavy structure, I'd pour a deeper footing, reinforcing near the top and the bottom as well.

For your wall or house, you won't need all this information unless you have a problem site. I once laid a stone house foundation right across an old well, by using forms and deepening the footing with more reinforcing. It's still standing, I'm told.

Very soft ground or ground with some solid stone partially underneath means you need a heavier footing to reduce settling and cracking where there are weak places.

Figure 5-9 Foundation wall showing stepped, wide footing up a hill. Opening is for a basement door.

Figure 5-10. Before the coming of concrete footings, masons widened the bases of their chimneys to distribute the weight. This cabin chimney is of dense sandstone, dry-laid, near Cass, on the Mulberry River in Arkansas.

FOOTING SPREADS WEIGHT

Before concrete, early masons dug deep footings and laid large, carefully fitted stones to spread the weight and keep out moisture (Fig. 5-10). Sometimes they built on broken stone or gravel to allow drainage, down below frost line where water would run off instead of freeze. But there's always the possibility that more water will flow in and freeze above frost line than can drain off below. And a loose footing gets clogged, too.

Cover your concrete footing with sheet plastic, or keep it wet for about a week. Except in dry months, there's usually enough ground moisture to keep it from drying out, but keep the concrete wet whatever you have to do. A July drought can sap new concrete in hours, leaving you with a crumbly, expensive footing that does no good. But wait till it's partially set up to water it, so you don't wash it out.

A footing and mortar go together in stonework. Both are expensive and time-consuming, but both mean your stone structure will be permanent and solid. And you'll seal up all sorts of inviting crevices that the stone-dwelling denizens would find.

Figure 5-11. I like to use big stones in my work, partly because they require little more time to lay than small ones. Also, as in this foundation, they give visual variety and a sense of strength. Opening is for a foundation vent.

MORTARED STONE **55**

Figure 6-1. A stone foundation wall for a recycled log blacksmith shop in the Blue Ridge mountains.

CHAPTER   SIX

BUILDING A STONE WALL

STONE WALLS ARE HANDY as property lines, retaining walls, and places to sit, hide behind, plant against, and swing wrought-iron gates from. They improve greatly with age, dreaming away the centuries of their stones in the shimmer of drowsy sun. Almost everyone I know wants a stone wall some day, for reasons probably as real as the primordial rock caves deep in our minds.

Stone walls are so permanent, so *right*—most of them—that they look hard to build. Building a stone wall seems to be a craft reserved for the rare artist who can place the right stone atop another and have them stand forever.

Let's look into that.

So far, we've been pretty general, so you'll know more about the materials you'll be dealing with. Now we'll build a specific structure, the stone wall, which is really the basis for almost everything built of stone.

PATTERNS

Since we're building with mortar, we have a choice of styles: ledge (which you got into with drystone), random, rubble, or faced patterns. There are others, such as coursed cut stone (ashlar), but if you can handle uncoursed work, the straight-line work will be simple.

Ledge (horizontal layers) is the strongest, the way stone would occur in nature (Fig. 6-2). Random or uncoursed simply means you fit any rock into any space, still paying attention to nonalignment of vertical cracks (Fig. 6-3). Faced stonework is the use of relatively thin, flat stones upon edge against random stones or rubble, formed concrete, or even—heaven forbid—concrete blocks (Figs. 6-4, 6-6). You've seen faced stone on all those WPA schoolhouse projects around the country, often with the cracks dressed up with a bead of rounded mortar. It's always looked fake and still does, since rock just doesn't happen that way. Rubble is a non-pattern of whatever you can find. It differs from random in that you just put pebbles and chunks into any space any way, paying no attention to cracks or anything else. The creek-pebble houses, walls, and barns you see are frequently of rubble, which is often held in place with a slatted form while the concrete or mortar that makes up a lot of the wall is poured (Fig. 6-5).

I prefer ledge, with an occasional angled or even vertical stone to vary the pattern. If you're in round-rock country this is out of the question, though. And since you already know the principles of the

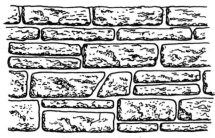

LEDGE PATTERN

Figure 6-2. Ledge-pattern stonework is that with horizontal layers, much as the stone would occur in nature. It is the strongest pattern for drystone or mortared work.

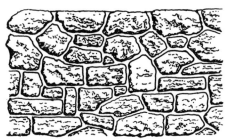

RANDOM OR UNCOURSED

Figure 6-3. This is random or uncoursed work, using odd-shaped stones and no regular pattern. The basic principle of covering each vertical crack with a stone still applies.

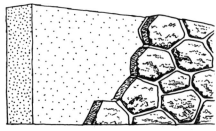

FACED STONEWORK

Figure 6-4. Faced stonework over another wall can be any pattern but is usually of thin stones laid random. Metal binders should be set into the original wall when it is built to anchor the face stones.

ledge pattern, let's talk here about the random-pattern wall.

Follow the rule of good masonry that each stone should stay where you put it even without mortar; look for flat sides and angles. Crumbly rock can be used here, since random means the use of more mortar and each stone is surrounded by, or floats in, mortar. You can also use two or more rocks to span the width of your wall, as long as you bind it occasionally with a single tie stone full width.

Figure 6-5. Pebblestone meetinghouse at Gilbert, Arkansas, a village built largely by a religious group after 1900. Apparently the gable was done with stone later. These are rounded pebbles from the nearby Buffalo River.

Figure 6-6. Peter Hunter lays stone veneer over a mid-wall framed in 2x4s and covered with sheathing. This was a post-and-beam basement wall, with stone fill between the beams inside. This wall is shown further along on page 50 and finished on page 167.

DIMENSIONS

Start with a wall of modest thickness, say 12 inches. It shouldn't go too high without angles, buttresses, or intersecting walls, but it's good for about a 4-foot height—more if the footing is good and there is an occasional strengthening bend to the wall. Four feet of height for the straight wall will withstand a moderate charge by stampeding buffalo. If that height doesn't give you the privacy you crave, we'll discuss strengthening for extra height in Chapter Seven.

Dig a footing twice the width of the wall, to a depth below frost line. As we said before, the idea is to keep water from getting between the rocks, freezing, and pushing them apart. Step the footing ditch if necessary, as discussed in Chapter Five, to keep it level (Fig. 6-7).

Reinforce the concrete footing with two ½-inch reinforcing rods floated midway in the footing. For a footing 6 inches deep, I pour 3 inches of concrete, lay the rod quickly while the cement truck driver fidgets, then pour the remainder. Cover the fresh work with sheet plastic or wet burlap bags for five or six days, to hold the moisture in and cure the cement completely.

Figure 6-7. This stepped footing ditch is ready to be poured, with reinforcing rods in place. It was for a stone foundation for a house.

LAY STONES!

Now you're ready to begin. The first stones will be belowground, so choose the least-cosmetic large ones. You will hear advice about laying the first course in the wet footing, which is fine if you're fast enough. Don't worry about it, though, since only that first course would benefit. Assuming the footing is cured, wet it before you spread on an inch or so of mortar and bed your first stones. Always wet the surface you're putting mortar on—not enough to wash it out, but enough to keep the porous stones from drying the mortar out before it can bond.

Just drop in whatever rock fits best, keeping in mind that you'll have to follow this act with another layer and then another. Leaving a peak on top means a lot of mortar, and possibly small stones, to bring everything up to a good surface to lay the next stone on. If necessary, use the small stone hammer to knock off offending protrusions. Watch our for flying shards. Use a chipping approach, similar to the old block ice chipping, near the edge. And wear something over your eyes.

Working at or below your foot level is murder on your back, so don't try to do too much at first. Don't set big goals just because you won't have another day to work till next month. No hand craft should be rushed. These rocks have been waiting around for you a long time, and your wall will be here long enough again to make any hurry insignificant.

Start your wall with square-ended stones, to give a vertical beginning. You may start against a house or a hedge, but keep the stonework neat. Use the level here; straight up is hard to guess on a slope.

Lay over a layer or two at a time, covering each day's work with sheet plastic or wet burlap. Uncover 4 to 12 hours later to brush the joints, then re-cover to hold the moisture in. Work on down the wall and come back for another layer or two no sooner than two days later. This gives the mortar a chance to harden partially and gives you a solid wall to work on.

Your mortar will disappear alarmingly fast on the first layer. You're laying stone on a wide footing, and it can spread out a lot. Scoop up large quantities that have dropped, but forget small bits. And don't try to save droppings that have dirt in them. All this up to ground level will be filled in with dirt, anyway. You might want to stretch a string to keep things straight, but belowground it's close enough if done by eye.

MAKE IT NEAT

Aboveground it's a different matter. All the neighborhood handymen will drop over to offer their observations and to criticize, and you want it to look right. That also means it won't fall down. I've developed a detached grunt for onlookers' comments which soon discourages them. You can also try a stone for size, reject it, and drop it near their toes for emphasis.

Here aboveground you will probably stretch strings for guidance, for both sides of the 12-inch wall (Fig. 6-8). If you let the stones touch the string, it'll get pushed off course. And you can expect the strings to get in the way a lot. I don't use any guidelines but my eye, stepping back to sight each stone from both end and side before I pronounce its location final. Gives me a chance to rest the back, too.

Don't mix large quantities of mortar if darkness or a rainstorm is approaching. Experiment with small batches, to see about how far they will go, and work out your own amounts. Be sure to scour out your wheelbarrow or box with a wire brush before you leave it. And cover your fresh work to hold in moisture. As we said, if mortar dries out before it can bond chemically, it will crumble.

Don't lay stone in freezing weather. First of all, it's no fun. Also, the freezing of the water in the mortar will mess up the chemistry. There are some products on the market, notably calcium chloride, to prevent freezing, but my experience with them has not been good. I have even wheeled my wheelbarrowful of mortar over a smoldering campfire to keep it from freezing, then kept a fire going near the newly laid wall, but I won't do it again. When it's that cold, I content myself with stone prospecting and gathering.

The actual laying of stone should involve spreading a layer of mortar about 1 inch thick and bedding the stone firmly by rocking it in place, which will push out some of the mortar. Trim the excess with the trowel, and use it in the space of about 1 inch between that stone and the one you laid next to it. With brick you butter the end before you lay it; with stone you work the mortar down into the spaces with the trowel. All the spaces are irregular.

Pointing up as you go means getting mortar into the joint from outside after the stone is laid, so that there aren't any holes in mortar

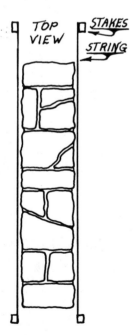

STRINGS STRETCHED ABOVE GROUND FOR GUIDANCE

TOP VIEW · STAKES · STRING

Figure 6-8. Strings stretched between stakes will help keep your wall straight but also get in the way. With practice you will be able to lay a straight wall by eye.

joints. It should be easy to flip small amounts in with the edge of the trowel, but it's not—only with a lot of practice. Get a little on the bottom edge of the trowel, near the tip, and smear it in with a pushing, wiping action. See Fig. 6-9.

A finished project always looks better if the mortar joints are recessed a bit, from ¼ inch to 1 inch or so, and it would seem easier to lay the stone carefully enough to attain this all at once. Again, it's not. The recess should be uniform, so that the wall looks as if all the mortar forms a flat, recessed wall of its own, with the stone faces jutting out.

So trowel enough mortar into the joints to ensure a good bond, and mix the stuff thin enough to hold, thick enough not to run. You can correct any sloppiness when you brush or strike the joints.

Stones may protrude a bit here and there, and this gives a pleasing rustic effect as long as most of them are aligned along the planned wall edge. When brushing out the excess crumbly mortar later, remember to strike the joint deeper around jutting stones to the same depth as elsewhere.

THE "RIGHT ROCK"

You will soon discover that you spend most of your time looking for the right rock, in this business of laying stone. Try for a dry fit first, allowing the inch or so for mortar. You'll develop a real eye for fitting odd shapes and sizes into spaces of the same characteristics.

After you've done stonemasonry for a few years, you'll be surprised how easy those aptitude tests are, with odd shapes that go singly or in combination into the odd spaces. And if you're good at these tests, you'll have less trouble fitting stones.

Use the stone hammer when you need it. Remember, though, that a fresh cut or break will glare out from a surrounding of aged lichened stones.

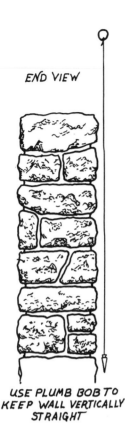

END VIEW

USE PLUMB BOB TO
KEEP WALL VERTICALLY
STRAIGHT

Figure 6-10. Use a plumb bob to keep your stonework vertical. It's particularly hard to guess straight up on a slope.

Figure 6-11. Trimming a cured stone for space to fit a foundation vent. Building codes specify where these vents are located.

Use the level or plumb bob to stay vertical (Fig. 6-10). This is hard if you jut a stone here and there, but you can step back and sight, with string or level held by a helper or tied from something overhead. Don't leave verticals to your eye judgment till you've done a lot of stonework. The weight of a stone wall that's off-center will topple it. And if you're going across a slope both front and side, it's hard to guess straight up consistently.

I have a friend who's building a hewn-log house atop tall stone pillars. His site is on a steep slope, and with allowances made for termite-height uphill, the stone goes up a full 9 feet on the downhill side. He laid it all by eye, and frankly I feared for its stability with that heavy house perched on top. He is, wisely, joining the piers with solid wall all around.

When you hauled your stones it would probably have been smart to stack them along the route of your wall for easy access. In practice, however, you'll find you do a lot of traveling all the way back, beyond, and around to find just the specimen you need. I bring a couple of wheelbarrow loads from a central pile to where I'll be working, before I start each stretch. Piled stone kills grass, limits walking space, and harbors noxious wildlife, so I like to keep it confined to as small an area as possible.

CAPSTONES

Even with a random stone wall, it's nicer to come out even on top. With this in mind, select capstones that have a more or less flat plane (Figs. 6-12, 6-13). If you've been conscientious about the inside and the outside surfaces, this means you need some really rare rocks for the top—more or less flat on three sides. You may want to switch to a ledge layer here, but this too means you have to think ahead and leave a good surface to lay the ledge on.

Evening out the top with mortar is to be kept to a minimum for appearance and durability. The mortar will chip and crumble away where it's thin, with the onslaughts of winter freezes, children's shoes, and walnut cracking.

Going uphill or downhill, I like to keep the top of the wall parallel to the ground unless it's very steep. Then you might want to step the top, just as you did the foundation. But do it in a series of small drops (Fig. 6-14). I've seen high-priced subdivisions stone-walled with heightening stretches of wall that drop way down, then go off again. I get the feeling that they're really big plastic panels with stones cleverly painted on. Maybe they are.

Remember one thing about your adventure in wall-building: It must look good. It's nice if it stands, too, but most likely it will. There's nothing as permanently glaring as sloppy stonework; it doesn't biodegrade well at all.

I'm reminded of a massive entrance gateway to a horse ranch in Arkansas that the owners had a local mason build. For days he selected and hauled perfect specimens of lichened, aged sandstone, stacking

CAPSTONES SHOULD BE FLAT ON TOP

Fig. 6-12.

Figure 6-12. Plan your wall to come out even on top, whether you use capstones or not. This will take some careful stone selection or shaping.

Fig. 6-13.

WIDE CAPSTONES HELP KEEP OUT WATER

Figure 6-13. Flat capstones keep water out of cracks in dry stonework and help tie any wall together better.

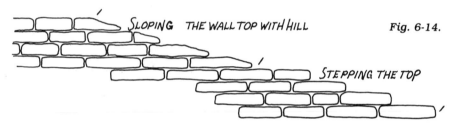

SLOPING THE WALL TOP WITH HILL

Fig. 6-14.

STEPPING THE TOP

Figure 6-14. The stone wall can be capped parallel with the ground or in steps. Steps should be set close and low.

it neatly at the site. He dug and poured a good footing. He even laid the ledge pattern carefully. But he smeared the mortar all over the stone faces and didn't brush it off—all that work and expense to erect what is probably the ugliest gateway I recall seeing. And after ten years it hasn't improved any. A total of two hours spent wire-brushing off the excess and striking the joints as he went along would have made that a handsome piece of work.

Don't get cute with artsy geometric designs, and don't put anything but stone in a stone wall, unless it's iron to swing a gate from. You've probably seen masonry walls surmounted by sharpened spikes or broken bottles, apparently to discourage trespassers. I hope you don't live in an area that forces you to consider this. Such ugliness says more about the individual cowering inside the wall than those outside.

A wall is for beauty—permanent beauty. Anyone who wants over it can and will get over it. It's for sitting on when the long afternoon light goes golden. Sometimes it's for a spirited horse and rider to clear, etched against the sky in an outline that never grows stale.

Think about the stone walls you've seen. There's a timeless charm, a comfort and nostalgic attraction to most of them, and a standing statement of the builder's craft, his patience, his art.

And you're going to have one.

Figure 7-1. On this steep site, the foundation wall was extremely tall, so earth was backfilled to minimize the effect. Also, several corners—part of the design —brace the stone.

CHAPTER SEVEN

CORNERS, BUTTRESSES, INTERSECTING WALLS

YOUR STONE WALL can't just go on forever. Sooner or later you'll want it to stop, turn a corner, or do something else. End it just as you began it, with stones chosen to come out even as you go up.

Cornering is simple, too. Just remember to lay first a stone from one direction across the corner joint, then one from the other direction, next course—or a header over a stretcher, with another stretcher over that. Try to find stones, or shape them, to make a neat corner. An occasional wild stone is all right, but make it clear that your corner line is vertical, so the whole thing doesn't look like a mistake.

Aside from getting your wall to change directions, the corner will strengthen it. So you can build a higher wall if you corner often. That might look a bit odd in your yard, so if you want height, consider intersecting walls or buttresses. Intersecting walls will create separated areas along your main wall, which might give you some nice effects.

BUTTRESSES BRACE

Buttresses are simply very short intersecting walls that strengthen the main one. They've been around since stonework began and are most conspicuous on cathedrals, castles, and other tall stonework. Sometimes they're dressed up as flying buttresses, which means they lean across an open space to brace the wall. Sometimes they have nice arches in them and look mostly decorative. But like all good architecture, their first job is functional: to hold up that wall. See Figs. 7-2—7-4.

The buttress needs a footing just as much as the main wall does, and it's necessary to tie the reinforcing steel in with that of the main footing so the buttress won't crack here at the joint (Figs. 7-5, 7-6).

Both the buttress and intersecting wall must be laid at the same time as the main wall, so that alternate stones can extend through (Fig. 7-7). These also must be the same thicknesses to match the main wall courses. You may build only part of an intersecting wall to tie in with the main wall as you go up, then extend it later. But take it all the way up before you leave it, and leave steps to tie instead of a vertical end. The idea is to avoid any butted vertical joint anywhere in your work. Steps will make it easier to start again, no matter where you stop.

It isn't necessary to take a buttress all the way up the wall it's supporting. I let it taper up and disappear into the wall wherever it

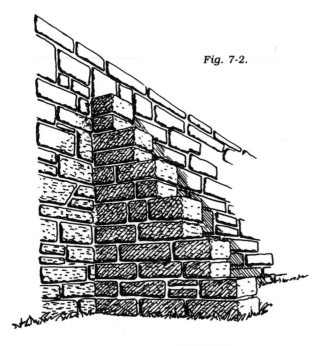

Fig. 7-2.

STEPPED BUTTRESS

Fig. 7-3.

ARCHED BUTTRESS

Figure 7-2—7-4. A buttress can take any of several forms, just so it performs the function of bracing the wall. These are the stepped buttress, the arched buttress, and the flying buttress.

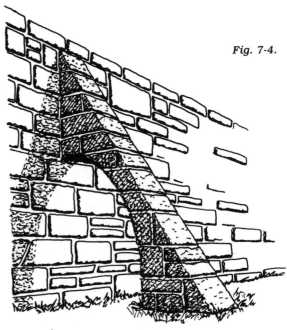

Fig. 7-4.

FLYING BUTTRESS

Figures 7-5 and 7-6. Buttress stones should be interlocked with main wall stones for strength. The footing under the buttress should also be poured at the same time as the footing for the main wall, and reinforcing steel should be tied across.

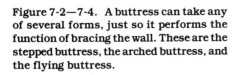

Fig. 7-5.

FOOTING DITCH FOR BUTTRESS

Fig. 7-6.

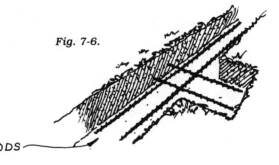

REINFORCING RODS

looks good, never leaving more than 2 feet of unsupported 1-foot-thick wall above the buttress.

I used a buttress to good effect on the stone pier to hold the bearing block for the waterwheel on the Turnback Creek gristmill restoration in southwest Missouri (Fig. 7-8). The pier was later incorporated into the wall forming the millrace and had to be 6½ feet high. I dug the footing in a T shape, then poured it with old long bolts as reinforcing.

In this particular application—a waterwheel—there are apt to be unusual side thrusts and twists if something like a log or tree limb gets caught in the wheel. The buttress gives it the rigidity it needs. Waterwheels should be stopped in winter, because the ice building up on them will tear them to splinters, no matter how solidly they're based.

I had occasion to test my work unwillingly one day when I slipped and got my leg into this wheel as it turned. Didn't quite break the leg, and I'm sure the stonework felt not a tremor as the 2,000-pound wheel stopped. Fortunately, it was a dry run with no water weighting the wheel buckets.

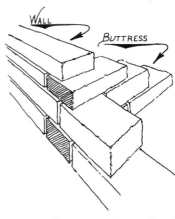

Figure 7-7. Buttress stones should be interlocked with main wall stones for strength. The footing under the buttress should also be poured at the same time as the footing for the main wall, and reinforcing steel should be tied across.

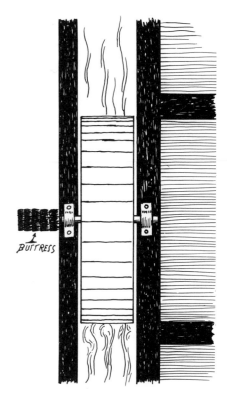

Figure 7-8. This is the buttress arrangement for the Turnback Mill wheel. Large limbs, logs, and sometimes ice blocks put heavy strains on the mill-wheel mounting, which should be braced to withstand them.

Figure 7-9. In this restoration a drystone basement was braced with concrete buttresses, poured one foot at a time to reduce pressure against the stones.

67

HOUSE WALLS NEED BRACING

A house wall will usually be at least 8 feet high and should require some strengthening. If yours is a hut 6 by 8 feet square, the corners will brace the walls, but if you're dealing with a 24-foot wall, it should either be thicker than 12 inches, have walls intersecting, or be buttressed.

You'll recall seeing old brick or stone warehouses where the problem was solved with a thicker section of wall every so often. Sometimes this enclosed a flue, but it helped widen the wall base and gave stability as well.

I've been particularly sensitive to strengthening stone walls ever since I watched a building being torn down several years ago. It was an old warehouse that had been gutted, with only the walls left standing to the last. It looked massive, with no cracks anywhere, the keystones tightly spanning the arched windows. I figured the contractor would have to dynamite it down.

He simply ran a cable in one window, around a section of wall, and out another window, and hooked it onto a small track loader. A relatively gentle pull bowed the entire wall, and in seconds it had come completely down. Of course the mortar used was lime and sand, which is weaker than today's masonry mortar, but that's not the point. You see, all that weight acts against you once it's off-center. So if your wall leans a little, you're in trouble. I've seen whole walls of modern stone veneer simply fall away from the frame houses they were anchored to, leaving just the fiberboard sheathing.

ROOF TRUSSES

If you have a tall house wall and your roof rafters, for instance, are pushing down and outward against them, they can actually push your house down (Fig. 7-10). You'll recall seeing those ornamental stars and other shapes of cast iron on brick and stone building walls, with what looked like rods or bolt heads through them. They are actually bolts, or sometimes bolts hooked to chains, going all the way across to brace opposite walls against outward thrust.

Of course, a roof should never thrust outward against the walls, but a lot of roofs on houses do just that. The roof should be a self-supporting unit, attached to the walls, not dependent on them for anything more than height.

Figure 7-10. These sketches show the thrusts of unbraced roof members on side walls. The roof should always be a unit that is braced to exert force straight down only, not outward.

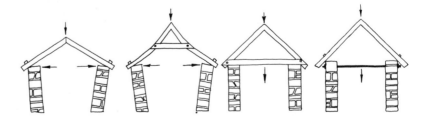

Figure 7-11. The corners in this high foundation help to brace it. The break-out for the bay window serves as a buttress.

CHIMNEY IN STONE WALL ACTS AS BUTTRESS

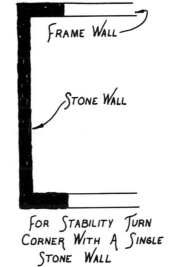

FRAME WALL

STONE WALL

FOR STABILITY TURN CORNER WITH A SINGLE STONE WALL

Figures 7-12 and 7-13. A fireplace chimney built into a stone wall can help brace it as a buttress would. Extending the stone wall around corners at its end will brace, too, for applications in which there is only one stone wall and others of wood.

Interior stone walls locked into the exterior ones help brace a house, too. They act as extended buttresses, although they tend to hold the walls out, not in.

A tall chimney would never stand without the corners to give it bracing. And the chimney itself can act as a buttress if it's built into a wall that's all stone (Fig. 7-12). For applications where one complete wall is stone, extend the stone around the corners of adjacent walls 3 feet or so for strength (Fig. 7-13).

Your basic stone wall, then, can be strengthened in any of several ways, all of which can be incorporated as part of the wall's beauty. An occasional buttress can have accent plantings around it and will give as good support as, say, an angle or a bend in the wall. And while lateral support is not a major factor to a low wall, it will be when you go higher.

Figure 8-1. The arched storage-level door at Sugar Hollow, a log and post-and-beam house I designed and built. This was a single-thickness wall, so we faced stones both inside and out.

CHAPTER EIGHT

THE ARCH, LINTEL, KEYSTONE SPAN

THE ROMANS PERFECTED the arch, using stone, and so significant has been its impact upon building that the word *architecture* derives from it.

An arch may span a stream as a bridge or form a window or door or fireplace opening. It may hold up the earth in a tunnel or be set on its end to hold back water as a dam. Its shape is as perfect as an egg or a planet, and you will find variations of it everywhere.

The arch is used to create an opening, while transferring to either side the weight, or thrust, that tries to fill that opening. A lintel (Fig. 8-2) also does this, but the strain on such a straight span is often too great to stand. An inverted V (Fig. 8-3) will also carry the stress to either side of the opening, but its sides are proportionately weaker than the point. The arch takes thrust evenly all the way around and redirects it.

A semicircular arch (Fig. 8-4) is strongest, as you can see from the drawings. Builders have played around with it a lot over the years to make it prettier. One major adaptation is the Gothic arch (Fig. 8-5), which combines the curve with the inverted V for a point. You can see that the sides of this arch are more nearly straight, so it is proportionately weaker here than the semicircle.

Another widely used adaptation is the elliptical arch (Fig. 8-6), in which the top is flattened from the semicircle. Here the top is the weak point. But as long as a curve remains, the principle is at work and the arch will do its job with relative efficiency.

You've seen old brick or stone buildings that are falling down. If the flat lintel is broken out over a window, the masonry will fall out until a crude arch is left, then it will stay put (Fig. 8-7). Artist Chandis Ingenthron, a dedicated caver, tells me that this is called a cantilever collapse when applied to a cave ceiling.

In looking at the way stress is redirected by the arch, you can see that the wall on either side must be strong enough to take it. The arch caves in if the base or legs can move apart. So there must be a massive wall here, or another adjacent arch, bringing stress to bear against the thrust of this first one. Stone bridges and aqueducts were braced with a series of arches—the bridges to let the water through and the arches to save the stone that would have been necessary for a solid raised watercourse.

ARCH SPANS OPENING

For your purposes, let's look at a simple gateway in your basic

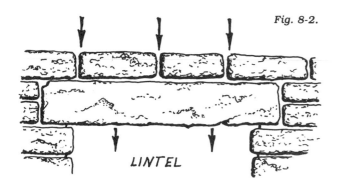

Fig. 8-2.

LINTEL

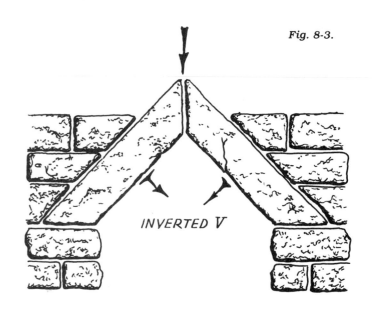

Fig. 8-3.

INVERTED V

Figures 8-2—8-6. The lintel and some alternatives. The semicircular arch is strongest, taking stress to each side from above. Both the Gothic pointed arch and the inverted V are weaker at the slopes, and the elliptical arch is weaker in the center.

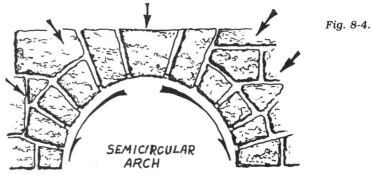

Fig. 8-4.

SEMICIRCULAR ARCH

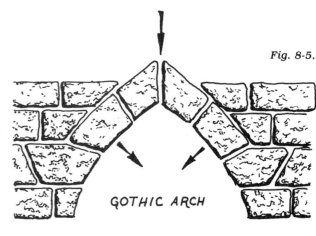

Fig. 8-5.

GOTHIC ARCH

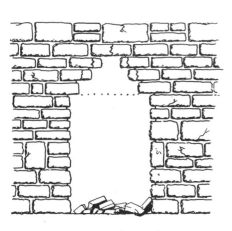

BROKEN SPAN TENDS TO FORM CRUDE ARCH, THEN STABILIZES

Figure 8-7. The principle of the arch is shown in this version of a collapsed lintel. Stones break off until a crude arch is formed, then remain stable.

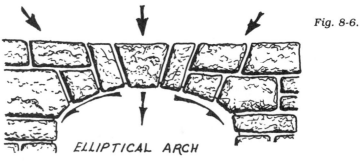

Fig. 8-6.

ELLIPTICAL ARCH

stone wall. We'll assume you have enough height to justify spanning the gateway in the first place, and we'll do it with a semicircular arch as the most efficient means. A lintel here would require a massive one-piece stone, which would always have a tendency to crack right in the center of the span where stress is greatest and under which your body, and other bodies, will pass often.

The keystone is the heart of the stone arch, more because it is usually built up from both sides than of necessity. Actually, each stone in the curve takes its part of the stress proportionately, and the keystone, being on top, takes just a bit more. It is not essential that an arch have one keystone as such; all the stones can be evenly wedge-shaped. I call this a multiple-keystone arch.

I use a temporary brace to build an arch, made sometimes of two pieces of reinforcing rod to shape it (Fig. 8-8). Anything will do that holds the stones in place till the last one, usually the keystone, is placed. Now lay carefully selected or cut stones up from either side, making sure each is wedge-shaped, wider at the outside of the curve. It's this wedging under stress that tends to tighten the arch, making it stronger. Once the final stone is in place and the mortar cured, you can take the temporary bracing down. I leave it up till I have several more courses of stone laid, to help lock everything in place.

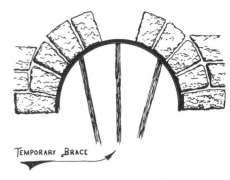

TEMPORARY BRACE

BUILD FROM BOTH SIDES TOWARD KEYSTONE

Figure 8-8. The brace that is temporarily set to form the arch upon may be removed after the keystone is set and the mortar, if any, cured.

Figure 8-9. Placing stones to finish the arched basement window after the structural course has set up and the form is removed. This is Gloucester Forge, a log, stone, and frame house in the Blue Ridge in Virginia.

Figure 8-10. A Palladian arch is a bit tricky, with no base for the weight. Here we've used 4x6 galvanized angle iron to carry the load to outside support. Stone to the peak of a gable like this is especially striking.

Obviously, stones must fit tightly for an arch to stand. Good mortar joints are almost a necessity for the arch; I'd recommend a drystone arch only if you cut each stone to fit exactly. We do talk about an arched drystone bridge in Chapter Fourteen, partly because it's so difficult to get a one-piece footing under a stream. I'm reminded of such a bridge in Lawrence County, Missouri, over the millrace of a now nonexistent gristmill (Fig. 8-11). It's a superb example of drystone work, using roughly shaped limestone only one layer thick on top. Been carrying traffic regularly for over a century.

Since the arch carries added weight to the ground on either side of the gateway, your footing here, if any, should be continuous. If you've tried to save concrete by breaking the footing under the gateway, you'll probably find that one leg of the arched opening settles more than the other and that the arch cracks.

In a bridge application, you can't very well continue the footing, so you dig deep on both sides, hoping for solid rock to anchor against. Lacking solid stone, you have to count on wide, deep footings to distribute the stress and reduce settling.

ARCH ADAPTATIONS

I usually adapt the semicircle for a fireplace arch, flattening it considerably so as not to use up too much vertical room. Sometimes I'll use a massive lintel stone here, but the arch means I can use smaller stones that are easier to handle.

We've used your arched gateway as a way to get through your wall. You might also build a series of arches to hold something up, like a porch roof or a second-story apartment over a garage or even an aqueduct or flume, if you're into generating your own power. Arched stone supports well, is more permanent than most other materials, and takes less stone than a solid wall would.

Another good application of the arch is the roof of a root cellar. Here it would be an arch extended the entire depth of the walls. You need extra strength to support the ground above, if any, as well as the truck that's bound to back over it sooner or later. The disadvantage to an arched stone roof is the likelihood of leaks, so we

Figure 8-11. Detail of drystone arched bridge in Lawrence County, Missouri, showing the roughly dressed wedge-shaped limestone stones of the 15-foot span. Built just after the Civil War, the bridge is still in use.

75

talk about the use of concrete in Chapter Thirteen on root cellars. But the walls of this structure, holding earth out, are stressed ideally for the outward thrust from the arched roof.

An arch can also keep the soil from caving in on a hillside spring— if you're lucky enough to have one. A spring usually means an underground open space, and at its outlet you need a way to keep the ground from falling in on it.

THE DOME

Closely akin to the root cellar or spring roof is the dome, which is a three-dimensional arch. For enclosing maximum space with minimum material, it can't be beat. The Romans loved it; so did the Renaissance cathedral builders and the folks who built all those state capitols.

Thomas Jefferson is given much of the credit for the Greek and Roman architectural influence in this country at a time when we were trying to be as different from England as possible. He became a master of the proportionate use of the column, and he used the dome to spectacular effect, notably in Monticello (his home) and the Rotunda of the University of Virginia, both at Charlottesville.

Even the Eskimos used the dome in their igloos. It's a natural form, growing from a use of blocks, whether of stone or of ice. The modern geodesic adaptations use different materials but the same principles of physics.

For your own projects, you would probably not tackle a stone dome, unless you wanted your root cellar to be round. You could build a stone igloo or dome to live in, but you'd have to plaster it all over to keep out the rain. The whole thing could be done much better with mesh-reinforced cement or almost any other material.

But arches, now—once you've put together a stone arch, you'll find lots of uses for them. They have become a natural function of the material and are a real building achievement, a study in classic building simplicity.

OTHER SPANS

Alternatives to the arch as openings in a stone wall are the lintel we've been talking about—no doubt the earliest span used—and the flat keystone span.

The lintel is simply a heavy stone laid across an opening (Fig. 8-12). It can support weight from above only in proportion to its own strength, gaining nothing from design as the arch does. The Greeks used the lintel to span their columns at the top, and because stone will effectively span only a short distance, they used lots of columns. Their simple solution to a necessarily longer span was to use a bigger, stronger lintel stone. And that's all you can do today, except maybe cheat a little with a piece of angle iron under it.

I will often support a lintel over a fireplace, window, or door with a piece of curved spring steel (arched so it exerts constant pressure upward). The principle here is that a straight support must begin to bend a fraction before its strength is used. It takes more strain to bow it farther, but that first bit may be enough to crack the lintel. Once cracked, the lintel is worthless, because it's dead weight. The arched steel support is already under tension when it's flattened by the weight of the lintel, so it supports before there's any give. This upward force can be in any degree up to the weight of the lintel, but any upward lift will help.

Of course, in the case of a fireplace lintel, you'll worry about heat drawing the temper of the steel and weakening the support. Actually, it takes a pretty hot fire to do this—hot enough to break the stone, anyway.

Stones above the lintel should be laid so that joints are near the sides of the opening. A joint in the center would put strain on the weakest point of the lintel, so the joints should be wide at first. Bring them in with successive layers, exactly like the pattern left by the broken-out crude arch in the falling-down wall we talked about (Fig. 8-7).

When spanning with a lintel stone, remember that the height of the stone gives it strength. A stone 1 foot thick and only 4 inches high won't have nearly the strength the same stone will have if stood up on edge.

I choose a lintel stone carefully, almost as much for appearance as for strength. It appeals visually to the same basic human need for shelter as do heavy beams in a ceiling. Overkill is impossible here; you need all the mass you can get. And remember, one giant stone is no heavier than lots of little ones, so if you can get it up there, use the biggest one you can find.

Figure 8-12. The fireplace at Possum Creek in Virginia, with a lintel stone. Seven of us placed this rock in David and Kathie Morris's log guest house.

A final word about lintels. This member should, for obvious reasons, be of dense, strong stone. Stone is so heavy in relation to its strength, however, that you're actually putting the strain of its own extra weight onto the lintel as you increase the size of the stone for more strength. This is why its effectiveness is so limited in stonework.

FLAT KEYSTONE SPAN

The flat keystone span isn't as strong as the arch, but it's stronger than the lintel. As with the arch, stones are slanted outward on either side of the keystone (Fig. 8-13). This means that to fall they have to push toward the center from both sides. The keystone wedges this side thrust, and the whole thing stays up. This span can also be built like a multiple-keystone arch, using evenly tapered stones all across. The principle is the same: Tight downward wedging of the tapered stones uses the force of gravity to jam things together and stop further downward thrust.

Because the flat keystone span is not as strong as the arch, I use steel bracing under it as I do with the lintel. If anything, this span

Figure 8-13. Flat keystone span, braced with angle iron over our kitchen window. This is triple-wall construction, with post-and-beam stone-filled inside.

requires a more careful fitting of the stones than does the arch, because there's no margin for settling. An arch can settle and still be sound, but a flat span is swaybacked if it settles at all.

Of course, the flat span needs a temporary support while you're building it if you elect to put it up without steel bracing. If you're framing a window or a door, the top facing, properly propped, will do to hold the stones in place till they're wedged. If you're using it over a garden gateway with no facings, just prop up a board to lay the span across.

We should mention another solution to the problem of spanning an opening, one used by most modern builders with brick or stone veneer: Don't span the opening at all, just stop the masonry at the top of window, door, or gateway. This is necessary anyway, if yours is a low wall. But a high wall will be considerably weaker if allowed to stop at the gateway and then begin again on the other side. In any case, stone or brick veneer work is so miserably weak, usually being put up over fiberboard nailed to softwood studs, that it would help little to join it over the openings.

Whatever your wall situation, you may want to build one of these spans just because you want to see this ancient bit of architecture in your structure and know you were able to master it.

Figure 8-14. Perspective drawing of Gloucester Forge, a house we built for sale, featuring high stone arches to support the porch. Much of the stone came from the property, with some 1500 lb. specimens used.

Figure 9-1. Much of stone's appeal as building material is in its mass, as highlighted by these narrow arched windows in our house in Virginia.

CHAPTER NINE

GATES, WINDOWS, DOORS

WE'VE DISCUSSED the methods of spanning openings in your basic stone wall. Now let's look at some gate, window, and door treatments you might use.

Your gate will require hardware set into the stone. Door and window hardware can be mounted on wooden facings, but these will rot if exposed to the weather outside. So will a wooden gate eventually, but it's easier to replace if the hinges and latch are permanent in the walls. I prefer a wrought-iron gate, which will survive you and me, even with little or no paint.

GATES

Make your wall end neatly at the gateway, using level or plumb bob to keep it vertical. Don't try to even up a ragged wall end later. The "cold joint" will always be weaker, and you're about to strain this part of the wall more by hanging a gate on it. So finish it evenly and build in the hardware.

The simplest approach is a pair of pintles set into the wall for the hinges. A pintle is a one-piece hinge pin with a mounting of one sort or another. On wooden facings the mounting is often only a sharpened point or a strap with bolt or screw holes. The hinge strap on the gate has a loop or hole that slips over the pintle.

For our purposes, the pintle mounting should be a strap or plate extending back into the mortar between stones. If it's strap, it should have a bend or two to help hold it in place (Fig. 9-4). If it's a plate, I like to cut or punch at least ¾-inch holes in it so the mortar can flow through and lock it in place (Fig. 9-5).

The pintle should be mounted with the pin upward so the gate can be set onto it. If yours is a wooden gate, it's a good idea to set the entire hinge into the wall, first riveting the pin. Riveting is done to make it harder for the gate to be lifted off if someone wants in when you don't want him in (or if someone wants your graceful wrought iron gate for himself). Hang the gate itself after the wall is complete.

If yours is an iron gate the best course is to set the pintles, then mount the gate after your wall is built. You can rivet the pins, heating them first. I use a welding torch, then hold a sledgehammer head under the pintle while I mushroom the pin with the ball of a ball-peen hammer. See Fig. 9-2.

Theoretically, you could set the entire gate—hinges, pintles and all—as you lay stone. But you'll find that you knock the gate over

Figure 9-2. Riveting the hinge pintle to hang a wrought-iron gate can be done with a sledge hammer underneath and a ball-peen hammer, preferably after heating the pintle end to red heat with a welding torch.

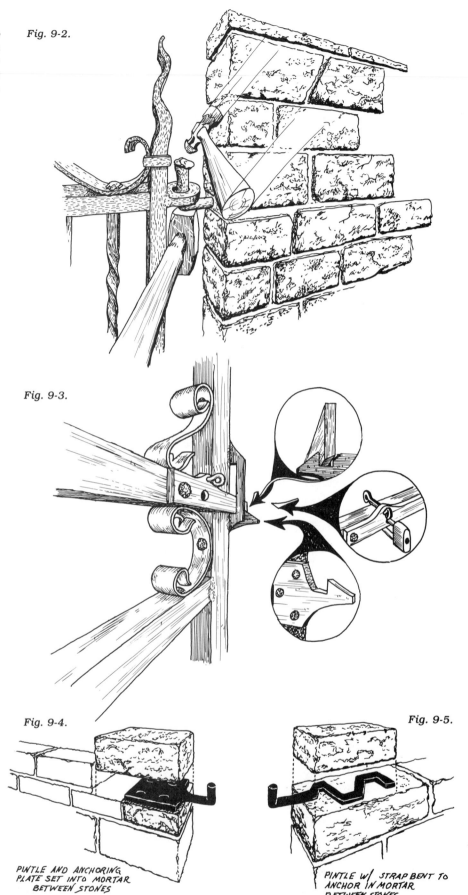

Fig. 9-2.

Fig. 9-3.

Figure 9-3. A wrought-iron version of the old wooden latchstring latch is ideal for gates. The bar can be lifted easily or locked with a padlock through aligning holes.

Fig. 9-4.

Fig. 9-5.

PINTLE AND ANCHORING PLATE SET INTO MORTAR BETWEEN STONES

PINTLE W/ STRAP BENT TO ANCHOR IN MORTAR BETWEEN STONES

Figures 9-4 and 9-5. Two types of pintles for gate hinges, to be set into the mortar between stones. The plate with holes in it lets mortar flow through to help lock it in place.

often and that laying two even wall ends is much harder with a gate propped up in your way. Of course, if security's no problem, just slip the gate hinge strap loops over the pintles and go back to your meditating. If you're into livestock, however, you should know that even an exceptionally dense horse can get the hang of unhanging your gate by nudging it up off the pintles.

Probably the simplest latch is an iron version of the old log cabin latchstring pivoting bar and hook (Fig. 9-3). The pioneers locked it from the inside by pulling in the latchstring so the bar couldn't be lifted from outside. On a gate it makes more sense to have a knob or handle of sorts to lift by, both inside and out. The gate can be locked with a padlock through matching holes in the bar and the gate itself.

Commercial hardware is available for your gate, but I suspect you'd be happier with something handmade. If you're not inclined that way yourself, look around for a blacksmith. Quite a few young craftsmen are learning this old trade for the needs of discerning folks; you can find one through magazine ads, if no other way. Or visit a local welding shop and have something put together there. Paint your ironwork, preferably a flat black. Modern mild steel doesn't turn black and endure like the real wrought iron our ancestors had for their hardware, so it will rust if not painted.

WINDOW AND DOOR FACINGS

Windows and doors should be mounted on facings. I use a subfacing of 2-inch-thick wood against the stone wall, then nail the finish facing it. Anchoring bolts or spikes can be used, countersunk so the finish facing covers them.

So that I can tighten the facings when they dry out and get loose, I use bolts with the nuts countersunk into the 2-inch facing. Sometimes I brace the facings in place before I lay up the wall, then drill holes and set the bolts between stones into the mortar. Other times I just set the bolts into the mortar, then put in the facing later. I put at least a 90-degree bend in the bolts to help hold them when the mortar sets up. See Fig. 9-6.

The windows and doors may be of any design, fastened to the facings as in a frame house. If a flat keystone span or a lintel is used overhead, the steel support is best bolted to the top subfacing. The ends of the steel bracing go into the mortar between stones. Remember that an arch doesn't require the steel bracing.

Anchoring the facings securely is particularly important for doors. The vibrations caused by slamming a door can eventually disintegrate mortar and loosen the facings. Use lots of nuts and bolts—say a dozen for each 7-foot vertical facing—and set them deep. I use 10-inch bolts, 3/8 inch in diameter to anchor a 2-inch facing, and bend them for better holding in the mortar. Since you don't need the bolt head, it's cheaper to buy 3/8-inch mild steel rod and thread and bend it yourself. See Fig. 9-7.

When the wall is finished and all the moisture has dried out of

Figure 9-7. I'm mortaring in a facing anchor bolt in this basement doorway after the stone was laid and spaces were left for them. These facings will be pressure-treated 2x10s.

Figure 9-8. Stone gateposts add a look of massive beauty to a non-stone horse fence in Virginia.

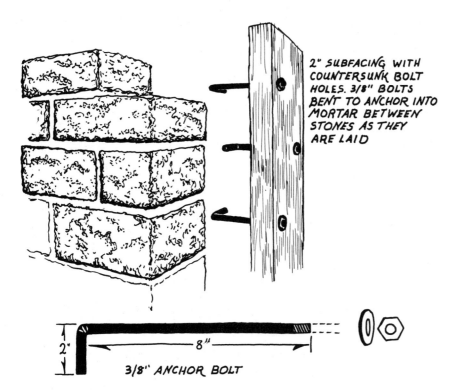

2" SUBFACING WITH COUNTERSUNK BOLT HOLES. 3/8" BOLTS BENT TO ANCHOR INTO MORTAR BETWEEN STONES AS THEY ARE LAID

2"

8"

3/8" ANCHOR BOLT

Figure 9-6. Door and window facings are best bolted to the masonry. Threaded rods or bolts with at least one bend in them are set into the rock, with countersunk holes for the nuts. Then a finish facing is nailed over the rough facing.

the facings, you'll find some slack in the bolts. Tighten the nuts now, and again before you nail the finish facing over.

Some masons use spikes, driven through and bent, to anchor the facings. This leaves no way to tighten them, and I've seen more than one house with loose door and window facings because of it.

A final word: You're going through a big investment in time, energy, and craftsmanship to create a structure of stone. Don't cheapen it with the quickie plasticized or aluminized offerings of the local building supply house. Most of the stuff available on today's market seems to be in a contest to see how flimsy it can be and still hold together till you get it home.

Don't disgrace your own craft. Seek out good stuff for your building from house-wrecking yards, antiques shops, and the workshops of other craftspeople. Try to find wood, glass, and iron that will look as good and last as long as your own work.

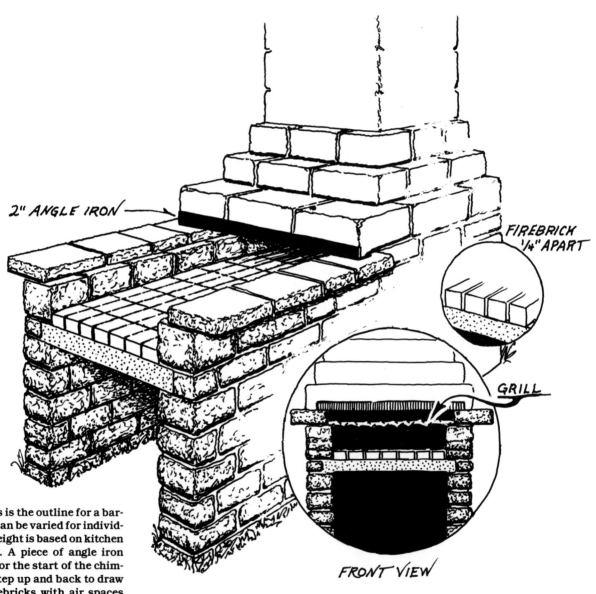

2" ANGLE IRON

FIREBRICK
¼" APART

GRILL

FRONT VIEW

Figure 10-1. This is the outline for a barbecue pit, which can be varied for individual preference. Height is based on kitchen
appliance height. A piece of angle iron
forms the brace for the start of the chimney, which will step up and back to draw
smoke away. Firebricks with air spaces
between make a good base for the fire.
They can be raised with another layer
under to get the heat closer to the grill.

BUILDING A BARBECUE PIT

HERE IS A STONE STRUCTURE that can become the center of back-yard gatherings and socializing with much more style than those tin washbasins on legs that smell of burned paint, or even those cast metal orbs that look like stray spacemen or rigid jack-o'-lanterns. A well-designed and carefully built stone barbecue pit will be the focal point of your patio, yard, or any natural setting you may have.

I'm sure the term *pit* comes from the historic practice of building the roasting fire in a hole in the ground, to spit the ox, pig, or game over, or of burying the meat in a hole lined with hot coals or rocks. We've refined this approach to burned meat, so that the modern pit is actually a fireplace with the fire out on the hearth. There are usually raised sides to the fire area to help contain it, and the fire itself extends back under the chimney to help draw the smoke away and up out of your eyes.

The idea of chimneys in the dwelling houses of common folks goes back at least to the fifteenth century, when they finally had enough of smoke-filled rooms where holes in the roof gave the only ventilation. A chimney and an enclosed fireplace were the answer, and these were located in different parts of the house. In Germany, the fireplace usually went in the center of the room; in Britain, at the gable end. In Scandinavian countries it was put in the corner.

Things were roasted in the fireplace until well into the nineteenth century, when the cast-iron cookstove became common. I am always taken aback by the primitive cooking arrangements in even the most elegant mansions of only 150 years ago. Food was usually cooked away from the main house, to cut down the chances of fire and to keep grease, smoke, and heat from the finer appointments. Thomas Jefferson's Monticello in Virginia comes to mind, that architectural masterpiece with its multiple innovations for comfort and its primitive, half-underground kitchen. Food no doubt retained its heat on the way to the distant dining table only in proportion to the swiftness of the servant bearing it.

In New England, at least, the kitchen fireplace was right in the middle of things, which helped combat winter's bite. But except for the swinging cranes and spits, little relief came the cook's way for centuries. Even a raised hearth would have helped.

SPECIFICATIONS

So that's the genesis of our barbecue pit. And even though

you're not condemned to cook on your barbecue pit all the time, we'll make it more convenient. We'll have that raised hearth, to whatever height you're comfortable with. Kitchen appliances are almost universally 36 inches high, so if you're of average height and used to bending over cookery at that level, let's place the grill at 36 inches. That means the fire area will be 4 to 6 inches lower, depending on the size of your proposed roastings. You'll need more charcoal and a higher fire level for an ox than for a quail, of course.

A good solution to variable height is to line the fire area with firebrick when you build the pit, allowing, say, 7 inches beneath the grill. Keep extra bricks around, and use them to raise the level of the fire for those romantic barbecues for just the two of you. Save money by using plain brick under the firebrick (which is expensive) when you raise the level of the fire. Another approach is to build in horizontal slots to slide the grill into, in order to vary its height.

DESIGN

The actual design of the pit is a pretty loose thing. All you need is that fire area at a workable height, with some sides, flat-topped to set things on, a ledge to set the grill on, and a chimney of sorts to draw off the smoke. Here we'll discuss a simple design, which you can vary at will.

Remembering that most kitchen work is done by the womenfolk, whose average height is somewhat less than that of men, you might want a couple of inches more height on the barbecue pit. The 36-inch height assumes we're all the same average height and all the same shade of anonymous gray that simplifies things for the appliance manufacturers.

To have enough grill area to feed a crowd, let's plan a 2-foot square for the fire. Add 6 inches of stone wall at each side, and we have a 36-inch-wide base. Let's make it 5 feet long, which gives us room for a 24-by-36-inch chimney with 1 foot to spare. See Fig. 10-2.

Like all mortared stonework, the pit should be built on a reinforced footing below frost line. A 4-inch-thick pad is heavy enough here, since the structure isn't tall and carries only its own weight. Reinforce with 3/8-inch rods or welded wire mesh, about every 6 inches both ways, midway in the 4-inch slab. Extend the slab about 6 inches on each side, to total 4 by 6 feet in size.

Walls need be only 6 inches thick, and for this small a structure you can lay just about any pattern you like without fear of its falling down. Lay just the peripheral U shape up to about 27 inches high. Now prop up a couple of 1-by-12-inch boards or a piece of plywood level inside the front of the pit to pour a suspended concrete floor on for the hearth (Fig. 10-3). Extend the reinforcing rods out over the stone walls at least an inch. You could use an arch here, or a flat keystone span, or even a large slab of stone. But the heat will ultimately play hell with stone here, so use reinforced concrete. It'll have a layer of firebrick over it to soak up some of the heat, too.

It would seem simpler to use just a close grid of steel rods on which to lay the firebrick, or even the fire itself. The problem is the expansion of the rods, which would push the walls of the pit outward and eventually break the whole thing apart. You could weld up a sub-grill grate—which I did for one pit I built—allowing space for expansion, but the ashes fall through and get rained on and messy. It's easier to clean if there's a solid floor for the fire area.

For this floor, pour a slab about 3 inches thick here—1 part portland, 2 parts sand, and 3 parts gravel—with rods every 6 inches or so across and a couple front and back to tie it all together. This slab will cover the entire U shape. Trowel it flat and smooth, and cover with plastic sheeting for several days to cure.

You can extend the slab clear across the walls, but I hang it on by about an inch or two and use a narrower layer of stone to get past it, so the edge of the slab doesn't show from the outside. You're up to 30 inches now, so take the walls up another 8 inches, then step in an inch or so on the insides for a ledge to set the grill on. Set a piece of 2-inch angle iron between the two sides and halfway back; this braces the first stones that form the front of the chimney (lintel).

Now, another 2 or 3 inches is all you'll need of stone sides. I like to extend the top layer out to provide a broader surface to set things on, say 8 to 10 inches. Of course, these stones should be as flat and as level as you can make them.

Start what is actually a stone smoke hood across the angle iron brace (which should have space to expand at each end), and slope it up and back into the chimney itself. This will help capture the smoke, and if you do it in steps it will give you places to set seasonings, matches, and so forth. Also, you can mortar in hooks or spikes at the sides to hang things on, such as fire tools, spatula, and fork.

CHIMNEY

Take the chimney up to whatever height you think looks best. It's a fact that a taller chimney draws better, but there are certain aesthetic limits. Six feet overall is probably as high as you'll want your edifice to stand.

Set a layer of unmortared firebrick on your suspended hearth (or two, if you want a small fire closer to the cooking). I leave ¼ inch or so of space between the bricks to let air get to the underside of the fire (Fig. 10-1). Cleaning out the ashes is a simple matter of moving the bricks and sweeping out.

The grill itself can be something as simple as an oven rack or as complicated as a specially forged wrought-iron one. Stainless steel is easier to clean, and you'll probably want this type. You'll save money by getting a cast-off rack and building the pit to fit it.

On that subject, a blacksmith's forge is very similar to a barbecue pit, with the addition of an opening at the bottom for forced air. Take out the grill, slope the floor to the airy entry, and you'd be ready to cook iron instead of meat.

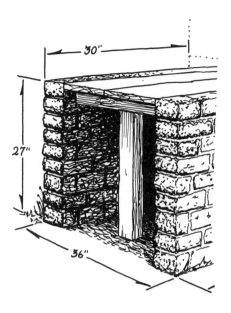

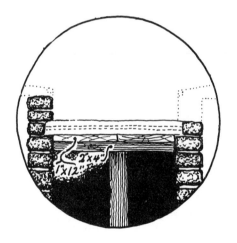

Figures 10-2 and 10-3. Temporary form braced from below is for a concrete slab that forms the fireplace. It is lapped over onto the stone walls to hold it up. Overall depth is five feet for the pit, but height is up to you. A higher chimney draws smoke better.

Figure 11-1. This fireplace has a four-foot millstone hearth. Stone is a combination of the local greenstone and a granite.

C H A P T E R   E L E V E N

STONE FIREPLACE

PROBABLY NOTHING you can build of stone will give you more pleasure than a fireplace. This is our most primitive contained heat source, and it is fitting that it be built of our oldest material.

On those raw nights when sleet drives into the marrow of the trees, you will soak in the glow from wood of your own cutting and watch the flames dance winter ghosts across stones that bear prints of your own hands. There is a primal response in us to an open fire that will never be touched by furnace or stove. And to have built that fireplace yourself gives it another magic dimension.

LOW EFFICIENCY

I am stubborn and bigoted in championing the well-built fireplace, and I'll continue to be. But it should be pointed out that fireplaces are shamefully wasteful of heat; most of it goes up the chimney. They take lots of wood and give little real warmth for it.

For this reason, you'll want to use all the ways to maximize heat output without losing the appeal of the open fire. First, you must understand the principles involved. The burning fire requires great quantities of oxygen for combustion, which then goes up the chimney with the smoke. The oxygen is drawn out of the house itself, through cracks around windows and doors and any place air can enter.

You can increase efficiency of the fireplace (or stove or furnace) by simply supplying a fresh-air intake from outside. Drafts disappear, and heated air is no longer drawn from the house just to keep the wood burning. This is best done with a vent right in front of the fire, ducted from under the house or from outside through the foundation (Fig. 11-2). This vent should be as large as you can conveniently make it, although anything will help. We have a 4-inch square Y passage built into our fireplace foundation that joins and comes up right in front of the fire. It's not large enough, but it's easy to see the effect on the fire when it's covered. A friend has an 8-inch-diameter duct for this purpose, and he says even that's not large enough.

It follows that the larger the duct, the easier the flow of fresh air will be, so make it big. A maximum would be somewhat smaller than the open passage at the damper (if any), since cold air coming in will be denser than hot, expanded air going up.

When there's no fire, you'll want to cover this vent to keep frigid air out. First we did it with a metal plate slid over the opening; then we put a small hood on it to keep ashes out. Now I stuff a crumpled

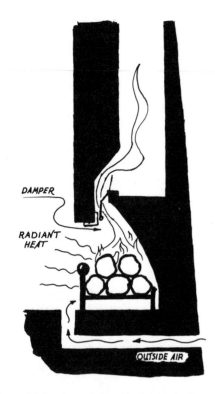

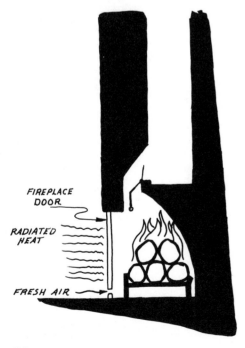

newspaper into it, until I get a little door constructed for the opening.

With all that heat going up the chimney, how does the fireplace give much warmth? It radiates and reflects heat from the curved back wall out into the room. Radiant heat is like sunlight; you have to stand in its path to feel it. That's why fireplaces bake that part of your body presented to the fire while your remote areas freeze.

So the trick is to minimize the amount of heat going up the chimney and to increase the radiant heat, while still giving the fire enough air to burn and to draw the smoke up the chimney. This is where the damper comes in. A fireplace without a damper makes a pretty fire to look at but little else. The only way you can get much heat from an open-throated fireplace is to build a big enough fire so that the very size of the constricted open passage slows the upward draft. This puts some heat into the room but consumes a lot of wood and is dangerous, since the firebox and chimney get much hotter than they need to.

This is the way fireplaces were for our ancestors for many hundreds of years—build a big enough fire and you get warm; cut and carry a lot of wood.

Figure 11-2. An outside air duct lets the fire draw oxygen for burning without pulling it from inside the house, which would cause drafts and take heated air from within. Heat is radiated from the curved back of the fireplace.

Figure 11-3. Fireplace doors should have a fresh-air intake low down if there is no outside air inlet. The doors absorb heat and radiate it outward.

REGULATE DRAFT

But it doesn't have to be that way. If you've had a wood stove, you know you must throttle the upward draft with the damper or all the wood goes in a burst of flame, the stove gets red hot, and you wonder how anybody could heat this way.

It's the same with a fireplace. A small fire needs a smaller opening overhead for the smoke to go out. A bigger opening pulls more air as the heated air and smoke rise, so you lose more heat.

Fireplace doors also restrict this upward draft, absorb heat, and in turn radiate it outward. Properly designed and fitted, they also allow the air to enter at the bottom, as your outside duct would, so that it feeds the fire instead of being drawn up over the flames and wasted. See Fig. 11-3.

We have an upstairs fireplace in our chimney that has one of those antique cast-iron fireboxes with a heavy front, which we sometimes use. This radiates heat nicely from a small blaze and helps get the fire started by keeping the intake air low and directed to the flames.

HEAT EXCHANGERS

Metal, double-walled fireboxes (Fig. 11-6) let heated air be convected or blown into the room, salvaging more of the heat produced by burning a given amount of wood. Their intakes are usually located low on the fireplace itself, which is poor engineering, since only a small area of the room gets the circulated air.

If these intakes are ducted to the far side of the room, the heated

FLUE TILE

BRICK THROAT PARGED WITH PLASTER AND FIRECLAY

LINTEL

ANGLE IRON

DAMPER

STONE FACE EXTENDS PAST BRICK

HEARTH

SMOKE SHELF

MASONRY TIES JOIN BRICK AND STONE

FIREBRICK BASE, BACK, AND SIDES

CHIMNEY BASE

FLUE TILE

PARGING

LEAVE SPACE FOR EXPANSION

DAMPER

FACE STONE COVERS BRICK

ANGLED SIDES

ARCH LIP WELL BELOW DAMPER

SLOPED BACK

Figures 11-4 and 11-5. This cutaway side view shows the modified Rumford fireplace we build. It has a firebrick lining locked to the stone with masonry ties, a pre-made cast-iron damper, and a smoke throat above the shelf to support flue tile and better direct the smoke. Front view below shows angled sides and the outline of stone arch facing the living space.

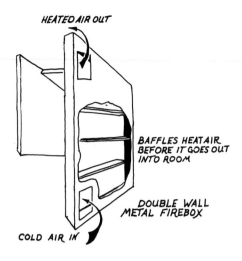

HEATED AIR OUT

BAFFLES HEAT AIR BEFORE IT GOES OUT INTO ROOM

DOUBLE WALL METAL FIREBOX

COLD AIR IN

Figure 11-6. A metal fireplace heat box, showing from side and top how cold air enters at the bottom, circulates, and exhausts into the room above. Fans improve the efficiency, but the heated air will rise slowly by itself.

air from the outlets will circulate farther to replace cold air drawn from here. Again, the ducts should be large to reduce friction. Blowers should also be used here, since the movement of heated air rising by itself will be slow.

Another heat saver is a heat exchanger of water-pipe coils which can be installed in the chimney to connect with your water heater or to a heat radiator. Forced air can also take more heat from around an enclosed flue into ductwork. I've never done either of these things, but I've seen them in successful use and I will add them to the next house I build.

So now you know some principles of the system. If you still choose to go with the fireplace, do so, as I do, with the understanding that you will never achieve the heating efficiency of stove or furnace, but you do know a little more of what you're getting into. We have enough dead timber on our 40-plus acres to feed our two fireplaces for many years without touching the annual growth. Then, with selective cutting of stunted, crowded trees, we're probably covered for our children's lifetimes.

BUILDING IT

Let's get on to the business of building the stone fireplace and chimney. We'll use as our model the traditional gable-end single fireplace, flush to the outside wall, which is also the easiest to build.

A chimney concentrates more weight on a small area than anything else you will build, so the first thing to do is get a solid, reinforced-concrete slab down for it to sit on. I've come up with a workable size that's double the area of your chimney base and a minimum of 1 foot thick, heavily reinforced. Your weight is concentrated in a C shape, so the trick is to make the slab strong enough to spread the weight over the entire area. See Fig. 11-7.

For a 3x5-foot chimney base, I dig a 5x7-foot hole to firm subsoil well below frost line. Next I pour in 3 inches of concrete, mixed 1 part portland cement to 2 parts sand to 3 parts gavel, 1 inch or

Figures 11-7 and 11-8. The fireplace foundation slab, showing location of the chimney base on it. The slab should be heavily reinforced and deep enough to avoid water freezing under it.

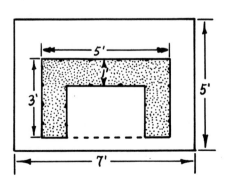

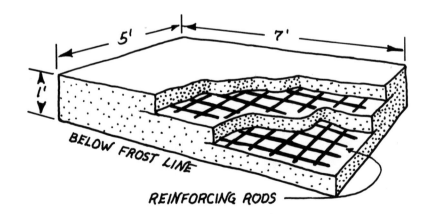

CONCRETE SLAB FOR CHIMNEY

BELOW FROST LINE

REINFORCING RODS

Figure 11-9. Beginning the stone fireplace chimney on the Virgil Culler log house in Bethel, Missouri. Stone is laid on the reinforced slab, and incorporates the end of the joist sleeper support at right.

Figure 11-10. With stonework near hearth height, the hollow center of the chimney is filled with broken stone and gravel, then a form for a poured concrete slab is set in place. This slab is reinforced with steel wire.

Figure 11-11. Beginning the kitchen raised-hearth pour at Culloden Farm in Kentucky. Fence wire reinforces, and a passage to the crawl space under the house supplies air flow.

Figure 11-12. Forming hearth support at the Culler cabin in Bethel, with air passage to crawlspace. Building codes specify thicknesses of masonry between firespace and wood such as the logs shown here.

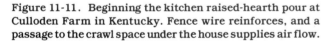

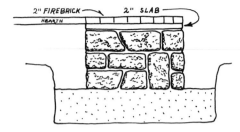

Figure 11-13. A second concrete slab forms the base for the fire area. A layer of firebrick brings the level up even with the hearth.

The back wall of the firebox can be brought forward in a flat slope, after the first two brick layers, in a modified Rumford design. Whether this back is curved or straight, the lintel must be well below the level of the damper, nine inches or more, so smoke won't roll out into the room. Also, the one-tenth spacing at the top of the firebox can be accomplished with the pre-made cast-iron damper.

A pre-made damper can go directly on top of the brick firebox sides and back, instead of using angle iron and building your own damper.

Refractory cement can be used to bond the firebox, or a mix of masonry cement with fire-clay added to the mortar (about half the quantity of the lime) in the mix. Use this mix for the clay flue tile joints also.

under in size. Then I lay reinforcing rods ½ inch thick every 6 inches each way, to form a grid. See Fig. 11-8.

I don't extend the rods all the way to the edge of the slab, since they'll rust away in time. Stop a couple of inches in. Next pour 3 inches more concrete, then lay another grid of rods, then pour a final 3 inches of concrete. Cover with sheet plastic and leave it for a week to cure. I'm told my formula gives more base than I need, which is just the way I like it. I've had no trouble with settling at all.

This much concrete would mean about seventeen batches mixed by hand in your wheelbarrow, so I'd advise a cement mixer or ready-mix. Try to catch your ready-mix man with a remnant from a big job; this will be cheaper than having him bring you just over 1 cubic yard in his 6-yard truck.

CHIMNEY BASE

Now you're ready to begin the stonework. You should position the chimney base a bit toward the house from the center of the slab, because there's little weight on that fourth wall. The fireplace opening puts all the weight, from the hearth on up, on the sides and back wall.

Lay a rectangle of stones to create walls 12 inches thick up to 4 inches or so below the level your hearth will be. If it's to be a raised hearth, you'll go right on up past floor level. I leave the center of this chimney base open, then fill with broken stones or coarse gravel, incorporating any ductwork for fresh air. You can lay the base of solid stone, but there's no weight on the center from the chimney. If there's to be an ash dump, incorporate it into the base, too. These have never proven satisfactory for me, since they usually clog up. And since the wood goes in the front, it's not much trouble for the ashes to come back out the front, too. See Figs. 11-9—11-12.

Next, pour a 2-inch slab of concrete across the top of the chimney base, leaving whatever openings for air and ashes. Reinforce this with any sort of wire mesh—I use recycled wire fencing. This will be the base of the fire chamber your andirons and logs will rest on. It's to be covered with a layer of firebrick that will match your hearth in height. See Fig. 11-13.

CHAMBER MOST IMPORTANT

Now to shape the fire chamber. If you're using a metal firebox this is no problem; just leave room for it. If you're forming the fireplace with masonry, you'll bring in the sides and back wall to the shape you want. Side walls that angle in at the back reflect heat better, so thicken your side walls at the back. Allow 2 inches or so for a layer of firebrick to line the stone with. Fire will crack stone, if not explode it into projectiles.

Bring the back wall forward in a curve, as you go up with it, to reflect heat outward. This curve should continue until it comes within a distance from the lintel that is one tenth the height of the fireplace opening. So while you're building up the sides and back, plan your lintel. Most builders use a piece of heavy angle iron here to reinforce the lintel, since it now carries the weight of the fourth side of the chimney. I have used angle iron, an old road-grader blade, or a lintel of steel-reinforced concrete, laid as if it were a long stone. If you use steel, leave room at the ends for expansion with the heat.

The lintel that supports the weight here isn't actually visible, since you'll face the front of the fireplace with more stone. The visible lintel stone or arch is largely decorative, supporting only that stone up to the mantel or to the ceiling, depending on the design.

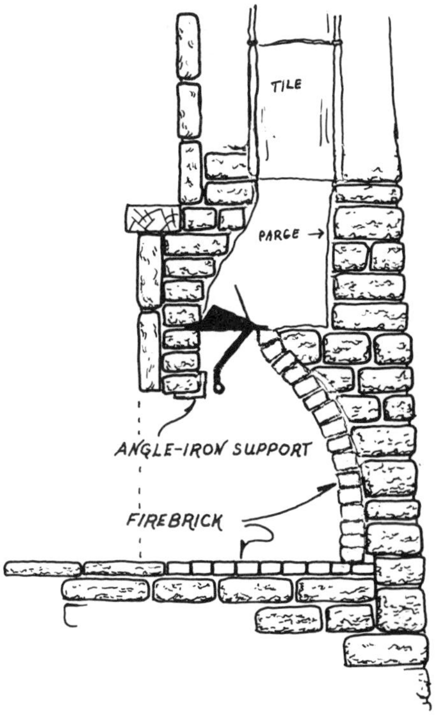

DAMPER AND SMOKE SHELF

The narrow chimney throat is where your damper will go. I set in a piece of 2-inch iron here to build the firebrick against; the damper can easily be hinged to this. The firebrick won't fall out if you've made a nice half-arch terminating at the iron, using the special mortar meant for it.

Bringing the back wall forward has meant thickening the wall as you go. Now you'll drop back to a 12-inch-or-less thickness to create the smoke shelf that keeps your fireplace from smoking. You will have downdrafts from wind under certain weather conditions, and this shelf is the best way to counteract them.

A metal firebox will sometimes have a built-in smoke shelf, which means your masonry can go more or less straight up. But sometimes it won't, so make sure the one you buy has instructions.

TILE LINING

Most civilized places have a code regarding chimney-flue tile—the city or county wants you to have it. Out in the back country you may be able to get by without it. It's chiefly for protection against flue fires. You see, soot builds up inside any chimney, but more so if it's uneven masonry. Smooth flue tile is easier to keep clean. Eventually a good fire can ignite that stuff, and you have a roaring fire inside your chimney. If you have a tin roof and there aren't lots of dead leaves around, and if your chimney is insulated from the rest of the house, you may be safe from a major fire.

Otherwise, use the flue tile, and get your chimney swept now and then. Chimney sweeps are proliferating with the return to wood heat, and they probably know more about how often to clean a chimney than anyone else. Also, some places require cleaning at specified intervals.

The tile is usually square or rectangular and is stacked above the smoke shelf. It should not touch a metal firebox; neither should masonry at any point. I mount the tile on angle iron set into the chimney walls (Fig. 11-15).

Support the tile by bringing the stone of the chimney in close here and there and stuffing fiberglass insulation in the spaces. Or you

Figure 11-14. Heavy angle iron supports the fourth wall of the fireplace at the lintel. Another piece of iron terminates the half-arch of firebrick forming the back wall.

Figure 11-15. Flue tile can be set on angle iron mortared into the walls of the chimney.

Figure 11-16. Firebrick is laid dry for the base of the fireplace. The flagstone hearth will extend out into the room.

Figure 11-17. The fireplace is lined with firebrick, laid up with special cement for the purpose. Sides are angled to reflect heat outward, and the half-arch curve is supported with braces temporarily. It will seat into the angle iron brace that is set into the stonework for it.

Figure 11-18. The finished inside stonework, which will support a hewn wooden mantel above. This cabin was built near the old Bethel millsite, so we built in half a millstone that had broken in dressing. Sections from the old French buhr stones were used in the hearth, groove side up. The crane, made from a buggy axle, came from an old Colony house.

Figure 11-19. I'm finishing a fireplace here in January, with a heater to keep mortar from freezing. Soapstone layer in firespace helps protect millstone hearth from cracking. Insulation goes between logs and smoke throat.

may fill around the tile with dry gravel. At the top you'll want to seal with mortar against rain, and you may want a chimney cap, too.

With flue tile, you'll have an air space around it to insulate the outside chimney walls against heat, whether you fill with gravel or not. If you build without tile, do use some insulation between your house wall and the chimney to reduce heat. Fiberglass with the paper removed will work.

If you use a metal box, insulate around that, too. The steel gets hot, and the stone around it is not a good insulator. The box also expands with heat, so leave spaces and pad with the insulation.

The flue tile can also be set on the brick rectangle at the top of the smoke throat, which is built up from the damper in front and the smoke shelf behind, tapered to the size of the damper. Also, the tile can be cemented directly to the stone walls of the chimney.

CHIMNEY SHAPE

Once past the smoke shelf, you have at least two options: Narrow the chimney in the traditional style or keep it wide to the top, which has been an earmark of fireplaces since the 1930s. A wide one is easier to build but requires more stone. Stepping it in is a bit more demanding but requires less stone.

Being a builder/restorer of pioneer homes, I always step a chimney in, either in steps as such or with an angled shoulder. Your flue will seldom be over 12x20 inches, so that gives you room to narrow things. I like to bring a 3x5-foot chimney base down to 2x3 feet at the top, stepping the sides and sloping the back evenly from bottom to top. I also taper the chimney walls from the 12-inch thickness up to maybe 6 inches at the top.

Figure 11-20. Dressed sandstone sloped shoulder of one of the chimneys at Turnback Mill house, Lawrence County, Missouri. Note the overhang to keep water out of the chimney. Rough pointing up is recent.

REINFORCING RODS

REINFORCING RODS

Figures 11-21 and 11-22. Steel reinforcing rods can help support the chimney at the shoulder whether steps or a slope are used.

Old-timers seldom reinforced the stepped places, letting the weight from above concentrate on the front and back walls of the chimney. I use steel reinforcing rods to help carry the weight out to the sides as well (Figs. 11-21, 11-22). These also make it easier to lay the step stones, since there's something to support them.

You will want to hang a plumb bob or two to keep your chimney vertical, and you should use the level often to keep courses true. Remember everything you learned from building walls about stones staying in place. It's all proportionately more important the higher you go.

Figures 11-23—11-25. (Upper left) Kentucky bluestone chimney at Culloden Farm shows flue tile, installed as the stone goes up. (Above) The trim rafters and part of the roof had to be sawn out to let the chimney pass through. (Lower left) Flashing sealed this joint against rain. On this job, Dennis Culler used a boom on his tractor to raise pallets of stone for the high work. It was necessary to raise the tractor on heavy skids for enough height.

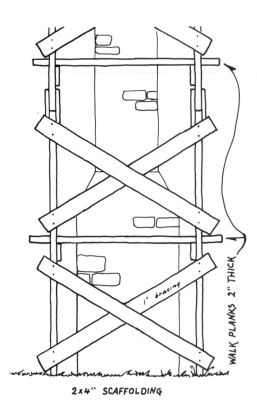

Figures 11-26 and 11-27. Scaffolding can be nailed together using 2x4-inch lumber and wide 2-inch boards to stand on.

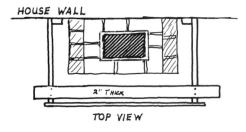

Building codes require a four-foot height above wooden shake roofs as a precaution against fire. Two feet is a minimum.

SCAFFOLDING

To get up there to work, you should have a solid scaffold. I build mine of 2x4s, X-braced, with heavy 2x12-inch timbers to stand on. Anchor the whole thing to the house if you can, because it doesn't take much of an outward push to topple a 20-foot scaffold, even if it has a wide base.

A tractor front-loader bucket is handy for chimney work if you happen to have one available. Everything you need can go into the bucket, which you raise to the work height. Then climb up and work from the bucket. Near the top you'll be out of the reach of most loaders, though, so you might as well build or rent a scaffold (Figs. 11-26, 11-27).

FLASHING

At the roof line you have to do some custom work with flashing metal to keep water from running down and into the house at the mantel. You will have cut out the eaves for the chimney to pass up through or have left them open in building. You'll seal to the roof on three sides with flashing.

As you bring up the sides of your chimney through the eave cutout, set flashing into the stonework above the roof. I let the mortar set up then, before I bend the metal down and nail it over the roof with washered roofing nails. You can bed it to fit first, then mortar it into place (Fig. 11-29).

The hard part is the house side of the chimney, with its slope. Set flashing metal into the stone in steps from the bottom, overlapping each one. Then bend down, trim, and nail to conform to the slope. Copper, aluminum, or galvanized steel will work here, though the life of galvanized steel is quite a bit shorter than that of the others.

You'll have a nasty time trying to put a compound bend in the piece of flashing that goes at the ridge peak. Most people cut it from the top nearly to the apex of the bend and hope. It can still leak that way. The best thing to do is cut out a close mock-up of cardboard and take it to a sheet-metal shop for a custom piece (Fig. 11-28). With part of the flashing cemented into the chimney, it's hard to replace it if it should leak.

You'll want to stop building on your chimney as soon as you can, but preserve till it's at least 2 feet above the peak of the roof. Chimneys work best at the ridge of the house, but if yours is elsewhere, be doubly sure to build it high. Cranky air currents around the ridge can drive smoke down the best chimney. A friend in Pennsylvania has had his restored house kitchen chimney rebuilt twice, and it still smokes. We blame high roofs nearby, since the house has had a town grow up around it.

A sheet-metal cap is good to keep rain out of your chimney. Rain will soon rust a metal firebox, and it makes it hard to kindle a fire any

Figure 11-28. The roof peak flashing piece, to be set into the stonework and nailed down over the shingles. This one was soldered together, of galvanized sheet iron.

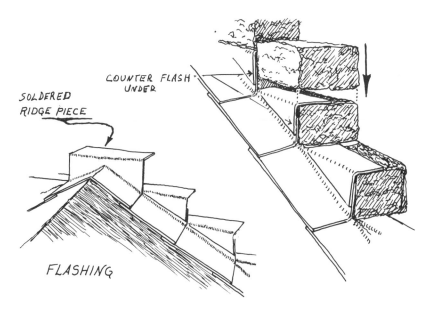

SOLDERED RIDGE PIECE

COUNTER FLASH UNDER

FLASHING

Figure 11-29. Flashing set into the mortar joints seals the chimney at the roof. The peak piece should be fabricated by a sheet metal worker.

time. Our own chimney sports a stone slab across elevated corner stones. Your may also want to screen against birds; chimney swifts will love your new chimney.

INSIDE FACING

I build the front of the fireplace, coming up to hearth or floor level from the part of the footing slab that extends under the house. Hearth flagstones can extend out over the subfloor.

Leaving air passages for the heat box, if there is one, I encase the house wall edges in stone and insulate them well. Once up to lintel height, make sure the two sides are even and strong enough to hold the arch or lintel stone. Remember that the arch will push outward as well as down.

The keystone arch (Fig. 11-30) needs no permanent support under it. A single, straight stone lintel should be supported with steel as a precaution. An arched single stone won't need support, since it can't fall even if it cracks through the center. I also support a flat keystone span, because this just isn't as strong as an arch. Angle iron is strongest and least obvious for this support (Fig. 11-31). Any piece of iron used here should have a space at each end to expand into with heat or it will make itself a crack somewhere.

The outlet for hot air from the metal firebox can be one or two openings, but it must be sealed away from the fire chamber and the smoke. If fans are used, they're best at the cold-air intakes; if heat-shielded, they will work at the outlet.

The mantelpiece design is entirely up to your imagination, since it serves no function whatsoever as far as fireplace efficiency goes. I usually hew out a heavy beam, support it on the stone above the lintel, and peg it to a log wall. If the wall isn't log, wrought-iron brackets of your own design would look good. Or you may want to extend two or more stones to set the mantel on. If you do this, be sure the stones are anchored by the weight of more stones above at the back, or by fastening to the wall. You don't want them seesawing and dumping your mantel onto a guest's head.

OTHER STYLES

That's your basic fireplace and chimney. For a freestanding fireplace inside the house or for double see-through, back-to-back, or suspended chimneys, the principles are similar (Fig. 11-32). Of course, you get no reflected heat from a see-through or suspended-chimney fireplace. A back-to-back is simply two singles, and the design is the same.

I prefer separate flues from multiple fireplaces, mostly to prevent smoke from being blown down and out the unused one in a bad wind. Flues can be joined anywhere above the smoke-shelf chamber (Fig. 11-33), which is usually cheaper than extending two flues all the way in the same chimney. Multiple flues are usually side by side, since that's the conventional shape of chimneys. Ours are front and back, with the upstairs fireplace a shallow one and the stone of the chimney walls forming both flues.

Building codes require separate flues, one for each fireplace or stovepipe thimble in a chimney.

Once finished, your fireplace can be outfitted with traditional andirons or any of several patented heat-saving grates that are available. I'd say squeeze all the heat you can out of the thing—short of boxing it in entirely as a stove, which sort of kills the effect. I, for one, refuse to block up a well-built fireplace to attach a wood-burning stove, no matter how it increases the efficiency. A stove is a stove, and it should be set up and operated like one.

But a fireplace. . . . Ah, that's another thing entirely. That's a *fire*place.

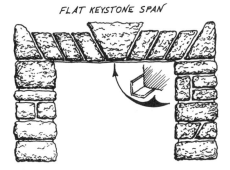

FLAT KEYSTONE SPAN

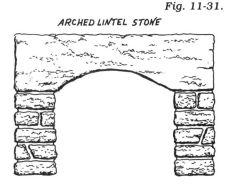

KEYSTONE ARCH

Fig. 11-30.

PLYWOOD OR WIDE BOARDS

TEMPORARY ARCH SUPPORT

Figures 11-30 and 11-31. Fireplace spans, showing temporary bracing for the arch, permanent bracing for the lintel and flat keystone span, and no bracing for the arched one-piece lintel.

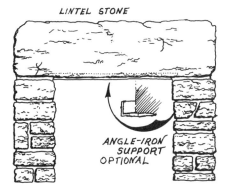

LINTEL STONE

ANGLE-IRON SUPPORT OPTIONAL

Fig. 11-31.

ARCHED LINTEL STONE

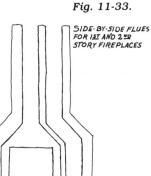

JOINED FLUES FOR 1ST AND 2ND STORY FIREPLACES (SOME CODES DO NOT ALLOW THIS)

Fig. 11-33.

SIDE-BY-SIDE FLUES FOR 1ST AND 2ND STORY FIREPLACES

Figure 11-32. Adaptations of the basic fireplace for multiple- or center-room use. Heat-reflecting properties of the suspended and see-through are nonexistent.

Fig. 11-32.

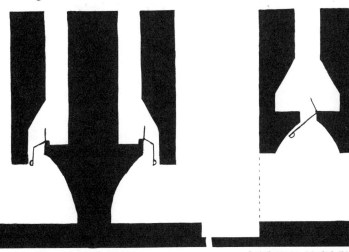

BACK-TO-BACK FIREPLACE

SEE-THROUGH DOUBLE FIREPLACE

Figure 11-33. Multiple flues can be built into a single chimney to accommodate fireplaces on separate floors. Above the smoke shelf wide liberties can be taken with flues.

Figures 11-34—11-37. (Above) Living room in the Fagan-Clayman cabin at Wintergreen ski resort in Virginia. Peter Hunter and I laid this random dense sandstone. (Left) My daughters Amanda and Lauren at the Culloden Farm living room fireplace in 1980. Flue thimble is used with woodstove. (Lower left) Kitchen fireplace at Culloden. Heavy beam mantel will be pegged to logs above stone. (Below) Den fireplace and wood storage at Greystone, in Albermarle County, Virginia, by Hugh Larew.

Figures 11-38—11-41. (Upper left) The living room fireplace at Greystone, where my style was tight mortar joints. Sloped structure at top is for upstairs hearth. (Lower left) Our Virginia fireplace is of mostly recycled sandstone from a West Virginia cabin. Second stones from keystone are cobblestones from Dublin that my longtime friend Bill Cameron brought me. (Above) This stone facing at Page Meadows, Free Union, Virginia, is to cover the ragged, unfaced chimney that replaced the original and had only the stove pipe flue. In 1859 the chimney was replaced and this space was covered with a fake fireplace and mantel. (Below) This is not a fireplace, but an alcove for the woodstove downstairs in the cabin at Wintergreen. Unlined stone absorbs heat, then radiates it for many hours.

Figure 11-42. I'm finishing the kitchen chimney at Culloden Farm. Stone lip at top is traditional.

Figures 11-43 and 11-44. (Right) Living room chimney at Greystone combines West Virginia sandstones. Screened opening halfway up is for air to supply upstairs bedroom fireplace. (Below) Dry-stone with clay fill on one of my favorite chimneys, near Cass, in Arkansas.

Figure 12-1. The terrace of Pennsylvania
bluestone slate at Greystone, a stone-
and-frame house we built. It is laid on a
crushed stone base with porous mortar
pointing-up to allow drainage and air to
tree roots.

LAYING FLAGSTONE

WE HAVE A FLAGSTONE FLOOR in our log house and like it better after five years than when it was new. Repeated scrubbings, waxings, and wear have given it an earth glow that belongs in our home. And with heat cable under it, this floor gives off a steady warmth in the winter that is the essence of comfort.

I recall my octogenarian friend Bill Cameron's story from World War I when he was with the Irish Fusiliers in the mud of France. "Sarr-gent," grumbled an Erin recruit to him, "when your feet's cold, you're all cold"—reflecting a moment—"and when you're all cold, you're dead." I agree. Cold feet should not be suffered in any house.

We have two fireplaces and, on occasion, a wood stove too, but the heated floor is our constant through the cold months. Its thermostat clicks off when the fires are roaring, but before dawn, when a bone chill creeps into the house, on it goes again. And our feet are grateful.

Flagstone was not a popular floor material for houses in this country's youth because it was cold and damp and the crumbly mortar would break down under wear. Today we use modern mortar between the stones, underlay them with a vapor barrier, and seal them with a masonry sealer that allows for waxing as with any floor.

Flagstone outside should not be mortared, since this will crack out with frost. Sand or packed earth between the stones will hold its own, eventually sprouting grass even if underlaid with a vapor barrier (Fig. 12-2).

NO SLAB

No concrete slab is necessary for either an indoor or outdoor floor if it's to be laid on the ground. Each stone will have to be bedded solidly in a layer of sand to take up irregularities in shape. Once set and leveled, the stones will stay put.

Our own floor is the third one of my building I've lived on, and it's built this way: We leveled the site, packing the fill by tamping and watering. (Water helps fill air pockets that would later allow settling.) Then we laid a sheet of 6-mil black plastic for a vapor barrier and spread 2 inches of sand over it.

Next some 800 feet of electric heat wire crisscrossed the main floor, and this was something less than a joy to lay. We finally drove nails the required 2½ inches apart, in boards laid down opposite walls, to string the wire on.

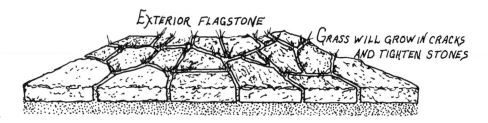

EXTERIOR FLAGSTONE

GRASS WILL GROW IN CRACKS AND TIGHTEN STONES

Figures 12-2 and 12-3. Flagstone should be set into a layer of sand so that each stone can be bedded evenly. For indoor use, a vapor barrier would go under the sand layer, with mortar between the stones.

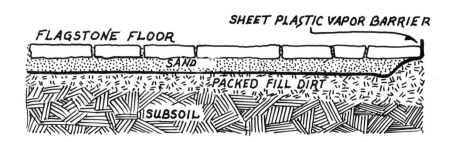

SHEET PLASTIC VAPOR BARRIER

FLAGSTONE FLOOR

SAND

PACKED FILL DIRT

SUBSOIL

Figure 12-4. Heavy sandstone flags form the porch of the Mansion House (1840) in Newton County, Missouri.

Then came the jigsaw puzzle of fitting the stones in. Since they were of varying thickness (you can count on this, too) sand had to be scooped out or added everywhere—no fun between strung heat wire. But this is not a job to be hurried, and if you aren't heating your flagstone floor, it's really not much trouble to bed each stone. We placed a few large accent stones around where we wanted them—such as right in front of the fireplace—and then started filling up the spaces, leaving about 2 inches around each stone. Leveling meant lifting nicely bedded stones a lot to add or remove sand, but, using large stones, it went reasonably well.

We had tried bedding all the stones first, then lifting them carefully out to string the heat wire and replacing them exactly. But of course that didn't work in practice. Sand got kicked in or a stone got turned and refused to go back in place. I will say here that my wife's patience was sorely needed and much appreciated that day.

Once they are bedded, walk around on your stones, putting your weight in the center of each, to settle it better without tipping it. Then, unless one drops significantly, you're ready to mortar the cracks.

MORTARING

Even masonry mortar will crumble under the wear the floor will get, so I use a straight mix of 1 part portland cement to 3 parts sand for mortar. Here the work won't be subjected to the temperature extremes outside, so the harder mortar is less apt to crack.

Filling will take less time and mortar than most of your rock work, because with 2- to 3-inch-thick stones there isn't much volume. Again, be careful not to tip the stones as you work. Trowel in the mortar, and trim carefully. This mix will be harder to clean off than the lime mix. And because you won't strike these joints later, they should be as nearly flush as possible.

An old craftsman I knew who built fireplaces down in central Arkansas always laid flagstone with a dry mortar mix, then used a fine mist from a water hose to wet it down. This way the mortar leveled out by itself and there were no air pockets. It's a tricky job, though, since just a drop too much water will wash out a hole or run mortar over onto the stones.

Once cured, your inside flagstone floor needs a couple of coats of masonry sealer if you plan to wax it. The first coat will disappear into the porous stone, but the second will seal well enough. If you don't plan to seal and wax the floor, expect it all to turn an indistinct gray-brown and prepare for eternal grit underfoot.

Furniture has to be pretty flexible to stand on a flagstone floor, or be made with just three legs. We use those canvas director's chairs and leave heavy pieces wedged level in place. Our dining table is three-legged, and so finds its own variation of level.

You could, of course, grind the stones gravestone-flat and smooth with a terrazzo machine, but that would be expensive and time-consuming, and would hardly leave you with a natural-looking floor.

Back outside on your walk or patio, your flagstone needs little care. Keep dirt swept off it or the grass that grows in the cracks will engulf it. Leaves and bits of grass decomposing will build up a humus to cover your stones in no time if not kept off. That's how ancient cities got buried.

THE STONES

The stones you'll need for flagstone work should be as smooth as you can find. Once laid, those boardlike stones will display hidden ridges, twists, and pits to annoy you. Don't be impressed by large, even-thickness slabs; once down, the only surface you're concerned with is the top. The stones can be from 1 inch thick up, since you'll bed them deeper or shallower in the sand to come out even on top.

Figure 12-5. Because the terrace extended from inside the screened porch at Greystone, we mortared between stones on all of the work.

Look for one smooth surface, and live with whatever's on the bottom side.

Flagstones are usually uniform layers of sandstone, laid down on the bottom of prehistoric lakes and oceans. We pry them carefully out of hillside quarries and haul them stacked on edge, holding our breath so they won't break.

Just about any stone that's flat can be used for flagstone. Ours is thin limestone from our creek, some of it in slabs as long as 5 feet. We were delighted with the odd pieces we found here and there up the creek when we bought the land. We prospected on upstream and finally found the wide shelves where the stuff had broken off.

We got permission from the property owners there to pry some more off and brought it home for our floor. It averaged 2 inches thick, and we had to cut some of it down to manageable size with stone hammer and chisels. And of course the uniform thickness that so impressed us amounted to nothing at all once they were down.

I have split layered stones for flagstone using several stone

Figure 12-6. The bluestone slate walkway at the Perrin Quarles house in Ablemarle County, Virginia. This walk and steps are underlaid with a deep footing below frost-line.

Figure 12-7. Splitting sandstone into flagstone with stone chisels or wedges. If the layering is clear, good flagstone can be had from several types of stone.

chisels along the splitting grain (Fig. 12-7). Once I located really good sandstone layers that we were able to pry up and use for flagstone—under 3 feet of river water. We also found that stone weighs less if you move it underwater. This flagstone dried out to be as sound as any I've used.

You'll find ripple patterns in flat stones, old water-borne sediment turned to rock by time. These patterned stones are nice for outdoor flags and steps, but would be a bit too uneven for inside.

FLAGSTONE IN THE AIR

Flagstone pretty much has to be laid on the ground for practicality, but it can be done on a suspended reinforced-concrete slab subfloor. You'll still need a layer of sand thick enough to take up the thickness variations. Such a reinforced slab with flagstone would be practical for a raised porch floor or deck that cantilevers out over your favorite view. See Fig. 12-8.

You just can't work fast enough to bed flagstone in wet concrete, so of course getting it into the slab is impossible. I did know a fellow once who built house walls of stone set into reinforced precast concrete. He did it by placing flat stones face down on a level surface and filling the spaces with a half inch or so of sand. Then he poured a 3 -or 4-inch layer of concrete, with welded wire reinforcing and heavy eye bolts for lifting. When it was cured, he lifted it with a crane and bolted it into place. The sand fell out, leaving joints struck evenly.

I suppose you could do this with a flagstone floor, but it's a ponderous business. Stone wants to rise directly from the ground, and no matter how bizarre the architect's fantasies, it's better used this way.

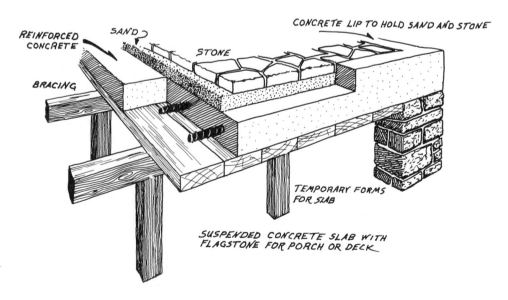

Figure 12-8. Flagstone can be laid on a raised slab, as in the porch application. The slab must be heavily reinforced.

Fig. 12-9.

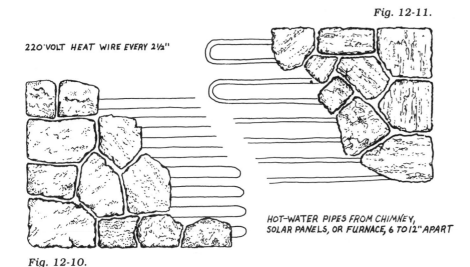

SOLAR PANEL

PIPE GRID
UNDER FLOOR

PUMP

INSULATED TANK
-ANTIFREEZE
SOLUTION

Figure 12-9. A heated flagstone floor using piped water from a solar panel. This pipe grid can be used with a heat coil in a fireplace chimney or furnace.

Fig. 12-11.

220-VOLT HEAT WIRE EVERY 2½"

HOT-WATER PIPES FROM CHIMNEY, SOLAR PANELS, OR FURNACE, 6 TO 12" APART

Fig. 12-10.

Figures 12-10 and 12-11. Radiant heat cable can be laid under a flagstone floor on top of the sand layer. Be sure to use a vapor barrier under the cable or the wet sand will conduct the heat downward.

HEAT IT

If you elect to put in a flagstone floor, give serious consideration to heating it in some way. The electric heat wire is comparatively cheap, working more like an electric blanket to warm, rather than like a furnace to heat. But electricity is an expensive utility and likely to become more so.

Hot-water pipes carrying an antifreeze solution from a solar panel or heat coils in your fireplace chimney will help warm your soles (Fig. 12-9—12-11). Store the hot water in an insulated tank and move it with a small pump; natural convection by rising hot water is too slow. If you do something like this and tie to your water heater, you'll have to use clean water, so don't go away for long weekends in winter without draining the system or providing some heat to keep the pipes from freezing.

A final word on flagstone, inside or out: Nothing dropped on stone fares too well, be it the family crystal or someone's head. We like thick rugs thrown around on our floor, and these take up some of the shock. But while an heirloom may just bounce once on wood, or cushion itself on wool, flagstone will surely crunch it up.

Figure 13-1. The icehouse at Jackson Mill from inside, showing fallen lintel stone. Walls are 4 feet thick.

ROOT CELLAR

THIS OLD BUT EFFECTIVE STORAGE PLACE is for your apples or potatoes (which are never stored together), and your squash, pumpkins, and canned goods. It's a subterranean storehouse that can double as a storm cellar during a bad blow. (Out in the country these are called "fraidy holes.")

Yours can be anything you want, from an earth-temperature cool place in the summer to an earth-temperature warm one in winter to store things. You can put in shelves for canning jars, bins and baskets, and barrels for other goodies. With a little light and ventilation you could even make yourself a workshop out there.

A root cellar is best dug into a slope, so you can get into it as nearly level as possible. This helps with drainage too, because you'll get water in it in varying amounts with the changing seasons. An 8-foot bank would be ideal, but you probably don't have one. Neither did we, but we had a 4-foot one, a hillside cut into when we leveled for our house.

So we had to step down a couple of feet to get headroom, which was no great problem. Also, we had to put in a drain to pipe the ground water farther down the hill. Our cellar top is even with the ground, and we have just over 6 feet of headroom. We could have let the top come up out of the ground and avoided digging as deep, but that doesn't give earth temperature, and we didn't like the idea of a funny-shaped stone structure there that would look like a mistake.

Let's say you have a bank or steep hillside, or both, near your house or house site. It's handy to have the root cellar close to the kitchen, because you'll probably use it to store food. If it's to be primarily a fraidy hole, you want it within bolting distance of the house when dark funnel clouds or nuclear uglies threaten.

SPECIFICATIONS

With this in mind, the cellar should be big enough to accommodate whatever it's designed to hold: potatoes, jars, or warm bodies. The old root cellars in my part of the country were only 4 or 5 feet wide, with maybe 12-inch shelves on each side, leaving just enough room to get in with a bushel basket. These went back into the hill maybe 8 feet. There were larger ones for prosperous farms and where apple orchards were numerous. The root cellar at the fallen-down house at Jackson Mill, near Ava, Missouri, was about twice this size.

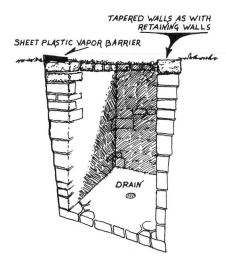

TAPERED WALLS AS WITH RETAINING WALLS

SHEET PLASTIC VAPOR BARRIER

DRAIN

Figures 13-2 and 13-3. Line the root cellar walls with stone as with a retaining wall to hold out the soil. A drain in the flagstone floor is a good idea.

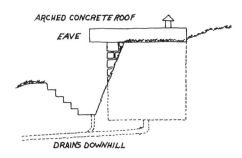

ARCHED CONCRETE ROOF

EAVE

DRAINS DOWNHILL

Also, along the millrace was an icehouse built on the same principles, with 4-foot-thick stone walls and earth heaped up all around it (Fig. 13-1). Ice would be cut from the frozen millrace in winter and stored here in sawdust.

For our family of four, living in the woods instead of on a producing farm, we decided that a 5x10-foot cellar was plenty big—not enough room for large gatherings but enough for a brief stay if the clouds threaten, even among the stored vegetables.

That meant, in our case, a 6-foot cut into the bank, then 10 feet 6 inches back, and down 2½ feet more. We dug a trench for the drain line, too. The 6x10x6-foot dimension was at the bottom; a hole always seems to widen at the top as earth crumbles off. That's good here, because your walls can be thicker at the top, as we talked about in relation to retaining walls (Fig. 13-2). I should say that this is no quick digging job. You're moving about 15 cubic yards of earth, or about 200 wheelbarrow loads. I'd suggest a backhoe.

MORTAR IT

With a root cellar you're dealing with an area entirely below-ground, with only the front and maybe the top exposed, so you're effectively below frost line and danger of frozen ground cracking your work. The pioneers laid their walls up dry, but here you can use mortar even without a footing—for strength, and to close up cracks snakes will live in.

Snakes love root cellars because they're the perfect temperature for them. A smooth wall of mortared stone is less inviting and provides fewer hiding places than does one of dry stone, so mortar. Sealed up tight, though, your cellar will be all right. (I mean really *tight*. A snake can get through a crack you'd think your knife blade couldn't.)

A 6-inch wall is plenty. Let it widen at the top as the earth bank recedes. Lap the corners with headers and stretches as we discussed with the basic stone wall in Chapter Seven. Bring it to about a 32-inch doorway in front and set in facings of lumber treated with creosote or some other preservative. You could use heart cedar instead, as we did here, or bois d'arc (Osage orange), or some other rot-resistant wood. This area will always be damp.

Assuming you've had to dig down for headroom, I'd say step the approach outside the door. That lets you shelter the door with a bit of an eave on top and does away with awkward steps inside. Of course rainwater and leaves will collect at the bottom of the steps, but it's a fairly simple matter to connect a drain to the line from inside. The leaves will be a chore no matter how you approach it.

MOISTURE

Theoretically, you can seal out moisture with a sheet-plastic vapor barrier, but some will condense no matter what. With ventilation—both intake and exhaust—you can keep this down. Do use vapor barriers at the sides, rear, and under the floor so the stone won't soak water out of the ground. See Fig. 13-2.

I like a flagstone floor with mortar between the stones and a pitch to the low point for the drain. Remember that your mortar work will all stay at earth temperature, around 56 degrees Fahrenheit, so there's no danger of freezing either it or your jars of beans.

ROOF

The roof is the tricky part of the root cellar, and the easiest way to build it is of concrete. You can arch stonework, as with a bridge, but it'll be just about impossible to keep a stone room from leaking. My advice is to form up an arched roof, perhaps using sections of oil drum braced from below or an arched frame of reinforcing rods every 6 inches or so, with boards laid on top.

Pour at least a 4-inch-thick roof, with wire mesh reinforcing. Build in a vent pipe, which can be 4 inches or so (plastic sewer pipe), to be capped and tarred later. Work the concrete with a pointed rod so that air pockets are filled and so that there's a good bond to the top of the stone walls all around. It's a good idea to form the lintel above the door, if any, right in with the roof. And let a few inches of roof overhang the door to help keep it dry. See Fig. 13-4.

Form the roof so that it completely covers the outsides of the walls. This way, water running off will go down behind the vapor barriers and less will find its way in. Cover the concrete with sheet plastic and let it cure for six days.

Hang the door as you would any door, closing against a weatherstrip nailed to the facings. The door is a good place for the air ventilation intake (Fig. 13-5), which, like the pipe exhaust vent on top, should be screened against varmints. Formulas for ventilation-area cubic footage vary with climate and the nature of what you're storing, it seems, but the 4-inch intake and exhaust works nicely here.

Arrangement of shelves and storage area inside the new root cellar is largely up to you. I am notoriously inept at growing produce, so I've never gone far into the business of storing it properly. There are good guides to food storage published by the U.S. Department of Agriculture, and publications like *Mother Earth News* and *Organic Gardening*. I like shelves down the walls for jars and general storage. Specific built-ins will depend more on the requirements of the things you plan to grow than on any standard pre-plan. Do keep a stool or two or a bench inside, to put a basket, sack, or your body on.

Stash some fresh water (changed periodically) and some survival rations in your root cellar for the day you lose your nerve and huddle inside it to ride out the rocky elements. Keep a Coleman lantern or kerosene lamp inside, since storms often knock out electric power. And remember that 56 degrees is pretty nippy for long periods, so have some warm clothes handy to fight hypothermia.

And come the terrors of black clouds or a bumper turnip crop, you and your stone cellar will be ready.

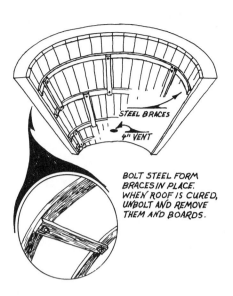

STEEL BRACES

4" VENT

BOLT STEEL FORM BRACES IN PLACE. WHEN ROOF IS CURED, UNBOLT AND REMOVE THEM AND BOARDS.

Figures 13-4 and 13-5. The roof should be concrete to seal out water. It can be formed over an arch, or incorporate the arch or lintel when it is poured. The air intake is screened in the door, and the vent pipe is the outlet.

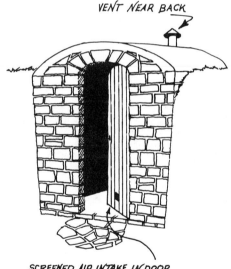

VENT NEAR BACK

SCREENED AIR INTAKE IN DOOR

Figure 14-1. Few stone projects can equal the beauty and ingenuity of a drystone arched bridge. You may call yourself a master mason when you have built one of these.

CHAPTER FOURTEEN

STONE BRIDGE

WHEN IT COMES to the picturesque, a stone bridge spanning a brook is hard to surpass. It tells of an age when builders cared about their work and took time to perfect it for both function and beauty.

The stone bridges of our country are fast disappearing, unused, subjected to neglect and the forces of frost, tree roots, and vandalism. They were rarely intended for the pounding and vibration of motor vehicles, and then only at a pace more sedate than that of our modern wheeled stampedes.

Lots of railroad bridges of stone are still in service, handling the steady pulse of the trains as they did a century ago. And you'll find concrete and steel bridges faced with stone to beautify the drab gray.

The National Park Service is good about using stone in its construction of roads and trails. I recall some very nice work around Gatlinburg, Tennessee, along the Little Pigeon River and up toward Newfound Gap.

One of the most impressive uses of stone to bridge was at the junction of the Potomac and the Shenandoah at Harper's Ferry, West Virginia, now largely replaced by modern spans. The old piers still rise from the ribbed rapids, true in quarried stone that carried trains for many decades.

PERMANENCE

Certainly the advantages of stone over wood or iron are obvious. Rot or rust will do in a bridge of those materials before the slow wear of wind and rain on stone. An iron bridge needs paint to protect it; a wooden one needs a roof to keep the rain off and high foundations to keep the beam dry from the earth. But stone can grow from the ground or the water-covered stream bottom itself to support roadway or path above.

YOUR BRIDGE

Let's talk about small spans here, the kind you'll be able to construct across your own brook or ravine, for foot or wheelbarrow use. A very short span of 2 to 3 feet can be made with a heavy slab (Fig. 14-2), as with a lintel. Remember that the stress is straight down, though; the slab must be massive to support a load on top of the strain of its own weight.

I'd use the arch on any stone bridge, for beauty as well as

strength. Let's say you have a stream below your house that runs in a 3-foot-wide course. You want a footbridge across it to your garden on the other side so you can wheelbarrow those tons of produce home.

Choose a spot that is narrow and deep for your bridge. Seldom is a path straight—nor should it be—so let your approach find the best crossing spot. If your hillside is as steep as ours, you'll have to

Figure 14-2. A single stone slab will bridge a small stream, but it must be heavy, dense stone for strength.

A HEAVY STONE SLAB CAN SPAN 2 TO 3 FEET BY ITSELF

Figure 14-3. Detail of drystone arched bridge in Lawrence County, Missouri, showing the roughly dressed wedge-shaped limestones of the 15-foot span. Built just after the Civil War, the bridge is still in use.

have switchbacks down to the stream.

If the banks are 3 feet apart here in normal times, you can be sure that the wet season will swell the flow beyond that. Watch the stream for several years to get an idea of how much span you'll need to let it all through. If you don't have that much time, ask around among the neighbors. If your bridge constricts the flow during a flood, it'll wash right out like a poorly constructed dam. Moving water is powerful and relentless, gnawing away at anything that restricts that movement.

If you've determined that this part of the stream never gets beyond its 3-foot-wide banks, you still want some leeway. I'd suggest a semi-circular arch 6 feet across and 4 feet wide. That would mean a peak 3 feet above the base, which should be set into the banks about high-water level. You'll need a filled approach to both sides of the bridge, unless there's a ledge already there at the right level, but this approach comes after the bridge is built.

DRY OR MORTAR

You have a choice here of drystone or mortared construction. As with all drystone work, you need to select or shape each stone

Figure 14-4. Although concrete approaches were required by the building code in Virginia, we used fieldstone in random pattern as veneer to help blend this covered bridge on the McGee estate at Fox Mountain.

carefully, because a tight fit is essential. If you use mortar, however, you must have heavy footings on each side of the stream, so that there's no settling.

The problem is that you must use two separate footings, and the chances of settling separately are much greater. With drystone, a certain amount of settling will not be noticeable, since all the cracks allow movement.

We'll do this bridge traditionally, as a drystone project (Fig. 14-3). As with all stonework, if you can do a good job dry, a mortared version will be simple. (If you want a mortared bridge, count on reinforced footings twice as heavy as for other construction.)

Dig a footing ditch to firm the subsoil at each end of the bridge. For the 6-foot span, allow for a 14-foot structure. So dig two holes 4 feet by 6 feet, starting 18 inches from the stream bank. Try not to disturb the actual bank, which will probably have roots and rocks and grass to help hold it. You may find subsoil a few inches down or 3 feet down, but I'd say go below frost line anyway to help minimize heaving from frost. See Fig. 14-7.

Now lay a base of thick, wide stones bedded solidly in the ground. If you have any irregularities on the bottoms of these stones, shape the bottom of the hole to fit. Lay this 4x6-foot area on each side of the stream at least 6 inches thick, then step subsequent layers up to the 4x4-foot base.

THE ARCH

You can see that this project will take a lot of good stone, so plan to do some shaping and cutting—more so as you begin to form the arch itself. Each stone will have a slight taper, like a keystone. For this span, we'll taper each stone about the same, instead of sloping flanking stones from the keystone, as with shorter spans.

Your temporary bracing should be strong enough to support everything until the arch is joined at the center. Four bands of $^3/_8$ x 2-inch steel, shaped to the arch and tied with bars between, would be ideal (Figs. 14-5, 14-6). I've used ½-inch reinforcing rods, again tied with rod welded between. Four rods spaced across the 4-foot width of the bridge will hold things stable. Bend them singly, then have short pieces welded between.

You won't be able to use small stones in the arch; ideally, each should extend the entire width. That's unrealistic, unless you quarry each 48-inch stone to fit, but you can get across with two or three stones. Remember that each wedge stone must be tight at both ends or one end can drop down and out when the temporary bracing is removed. It will take lots of chipping and dressing to get each one to fit.

The best stone for this purpose would be ledge stone of an even thickness. You can cut this stone by laying large pieces of it in sand and marking even widths with the stone chisel (Fig. 14-9). Now go along this line with a series of mild blows with the large stone hammer,

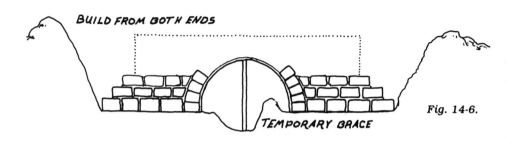

STEEL FORM FOR ARCH
3/8" X 2" STEEL OR 1/2" REBAR
CAN BE DUG OUT LATER

FORM ARCH OF TAPERED
STONES ON FORM

Fig. 14-5.

Figures 14-5 and 14-6. A frame of steel rods welded together supports the arch during construction. In dry stonework it is removed immediately after the keystone is set.

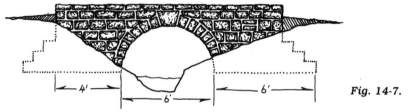

BUILD FROM BOTH ENDS

Fig. 14-6.

TEMPORARY BRACE

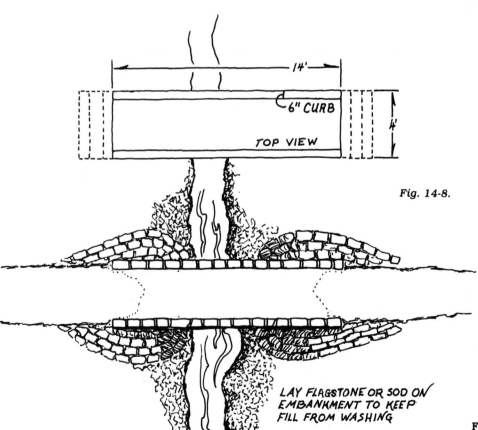

Figure 14-7. The stone bridge should span 14 feet, with an additional 2 feet at each end belowground for stability against the outward thrust of the arch. The 3-foot arch rests on a heavy, belowground foundation of drystone. Spanning 6 feet, it allows for rising water above the 3-foot streambed.

Fig. 14-7.

4'

6'

6'

14'

6" CURB

TOP VIEW

4'

Fig. 14-8.

LAY FLAGSTONE OR SOD ON
EMBANKMENT TO KEEP
FILL FROM WASHING

Figure 14-8. Top views show outline of bridge and footing; also embankment work to keep soil intact.

STONE BRIDGE **127**

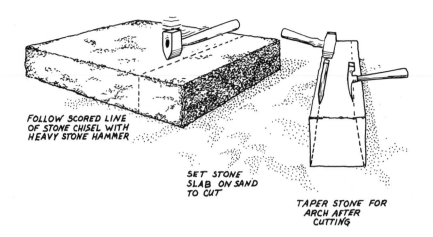

Figure 14-9. Wedge-shaped stones can be quarried for the arch using first the heavy stone hammer to cut blocks from thick slabs. Final shaping of the wedges for the arch can be done with the hammer and pitching tool or the small mason's hammer.

FOLLOW SCORED LINE
OF STONE CHISEL WITH
HEAVY STONE HAMMER

SET STONE
SLAB ON SAND
TO CUT

TAPER STONE FOR
ARCH AFTER
CUTTING

and again a little harder. Eventually you'll get a crack started. Although it may cut across or go wild, you'll usually get quite a few with parallel sides. Dress them further with the chisel or small hammer, which can also be used to get the taper you need. With enough searching among ledge stones, you'll find many that need little shaping.

Join the two structures at the peak all across, and then start subsequent layers over the first. You may want a level surface or you may want to leave it arched—either is strong. If flat, slope it a bit to encourage rain to run off in winter before it freezes.

FINISHING

I like to raise a low stone curb at the sides of the bridge to help keep runaway wheelbarrows out of the stream. You may also like to take nocturnal walks, and a bit of a curb can keep your feet from going over as you stargaze.

Fill in the approaches to your bridge with earth and scrap stone. You can sod the slopes on either side or lay flat stone up them to keep them from eroding away. The stone surface of the bridge itself can be made smoother by covering with sand and gravel, or with flagstone set into a layer of sand, using sand or earth in the cracks between stones. Or it can be left as you laid it. See Fig. 14-8.

As you know, a mortared stone bridge would require much less stone dressing, since the mortar fills in the irregularities. You will almost surely get cracks from settling if you build with mortar, but with the arch a crack isn't necessarily a disaster.

This type and size of bridge is a big, exacting job. It's the kind of thing I save special stones for over a long period. I have a lot of rectangular limestone along the streambed below our house that would someday make a good footbridge. At present we stone-hop across, because our streambed is 10 feet wide in most places and can swell out of its banks in minutes during a storm.

So if I bridge it, it will be in more than one span, to one or more stone piers in midstream. My neighbor upcreek raised a stone pier at water's edge on the sloping side of this stream to support a 50-foot span that goes from high on this slope to a vertical bank on the other. His bridge is of treated oak, X-braced for strength (Fig. 14-10).

By now you can see why most bridges are built of concrete and steel. I wouldn't tackle a stone bridge until I'd built several other stone structures first. Then I'd take lots of time to do it just right.

So why bother? Well, if you ever build an arched stone bridge over a flowing stream, you'll know why. And you'll know a lot of other things about yourself you didn't know before.

Figure 14-10. My neighbor's bridge pier of limestone from the creekbed. The bridge itself is of treated oak.

Figure 15-1. The gristmill foundation and mill dam at Jolly Mill in Newton County, Missouri, show good dry stonework. The stone dam is still intact, but the creek has recently gone around the end of it to cut another channel.

130 BUILDING WITH STONE

CHAPTER FIFTEEN

STONE DAM

HUMAN BEINGS have always wanted to harness waterways. The sight of all that energy slipping past on its way to the sea has awakened the inventive genius of legions of millers through the ages. Their end product might be flour, lumber, metals, or cloth, but first they needed power, to turn their machines.

And it came from falling water. George Washington, as President, urged the location of arms manufacturing at Harper's Ferry (then in Virginia) because the rushing waters of the joining Shenandoah and Potomac rivers assured lots of power. And some really complicated machinery was utilized to mass-produce muskets for generations of soldiers, all of it at first turned by falling water.

An engineer recently told me the most efficient storage of electrical energy is still the pumping of water uphill to a reservoir to let it run through turbines for power when needed. For a technology as advanced as ours presumably is, that's pretty basic.

Except in rare cases of natural waterfalls, or in situations where diversion is feasible, tapping water power means raising the stream level with a dam. Then you take water either off the top or from lower down under pressure, to do with whatever your scheme requires.

You may simply want a pond or a water supply and couldn't care less about potential power for irrigation, electricity, or motivating machinery. Yours may be a plant for a placid, landscaped little lake with weeping willows and a curving drive, while overflow water cascades down your stone dam unharnessed. Or maybe you want to stock the pond with trout, if it's spring-fed and cold enough, or catfish for your freezer if it's not.

You need a dam to back up water in a stream. And I should point out that, since riparian rights to waterways are sometimes complicated, you need to check into area laws before you dam anything that moves. Also, the federal government has its fingers in waterways of all kinds, so check your soil conservation office to see what you can do before you start anything.

KEEP IT SMALL

Don't plan to dam anything big, even if you find you can do so without incurring the wrath of downstream users, upstream users, or assorted bureaucracies. Large dams are such unnatural structures, with miles of water exerting constant pressure against them, waiting for the right earthquake to fracture something vital. And of course that lakeful of speeding boats drowns the finest farmland, in the name of whatever boondoggle its builders were able to sell.

But a 2-foot-high dam of fieldstone across your meadow freshet to provide water for your vegetables is something a little more between you and God. And for aesthetics, it beats using a bulldozer to gouge out a raw basin of mud and clay for the same purpose, which will take your lifetime to heal.

The dam itself is little more than a stone wall—mortared, of course, to hold water. For stability, it should be thick in relation to its height, and either arched against the push of the water or buttressed.

FIT IT TO THE EARTH

But the stone dam itself is probably not what will trip you up and allow your planned pond or power supply to run off downhill and frustrate your construction efforts—it's fitting that dam to the earth so water doesn't go under it or around it (Fig. 15-1) that will take some preparation.

First, you have the constant force of the impounded water against your dam. Then, during high water, you have increased force from faster flow and higher levels, plus possible limbs, logs, and trees borne down in flood. A large watershed can transform a tinkling brook into a monster in minutes during a heavy rain.

So let's minimize the force. One of the cleverest dams I've seen was the old stone dam on Turnback Creek in southwest Missouri, where we restored the water mill. Its builders had chosen an almost 90-degree bend in the creek for the dam, locating it just below, so the force of the flow was parallel to the dam, past it into the stone-lined millrace (Fig. 15-2). During flood the water spilled over the dam as backwater, and big things were borne past it. A screen of sorts stopped flotsam before it could get to the wheel. This dam stood for over a hundred years, until the 1940s, when fishermen illegally dynamited the pond and blew it away. At this writing it's being rebuilt to power the restored mill.

The Jackson Mill three counties east, built at about the same time (the 1830s), utilized a low diversion dam at a similar bend to direct the flow down the quarter-mile-long millrace. This race still crosses a side stream on a drystone bridge, although the mill is long since gone.

The overflow path from this type of location will have to be lined, or water will cut itself a new channel and bypass your dam entirely. Stones embedded in an embankment will hold, unless the water can get under them and eat the soil away (Fig. 15-4).

To get a good bond with the earth at both stream banks and at the bottom, you should dig well back and down (Fig. 15-3). Sod or silt or leaf mold will always leak. Dig below frost line, as for a wall or foundation, and dig into solid subsoil. To avoid cracks, you should have a reinforced footing, because in this constantly wet ground the dam will certainly settle.

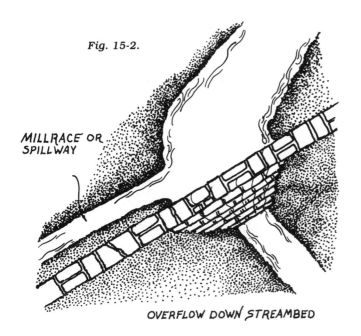

Fig. 15-2.

MILLRACE OR SPILLWAY

OVERFLOW DOWN STREAMBED

Figure 15-2. A good location for a small dam is just below a bend in the stream, so that high water force is down the spillway, away from the structure.

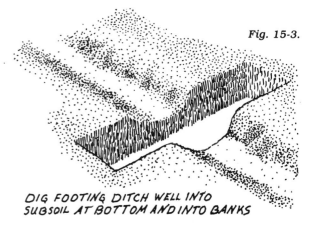

Fig. 15-3.

DIG FOOTING DITCH WELL INTO SUBSOIL AT BOTTOM AND INTO BANKS

Figure 15-3. Footing ditch for a small dam should be wide and deep, well below stream level in solid subsoil. Sandy soil or leaf mold will leak.

LINE SPILLWAY AND EMBANKMENT WITH STONE

Fig. 15-4.

Figure 15-4. Spillway ditches should be lined with stone to keep water from eroding the soil away.

Figure 15-5. The spillway channel of the Morah Mill on Spring River near Carthage, Missouri, is laid with stones sloped to prevent washing out by the water. Stream flow is from left.

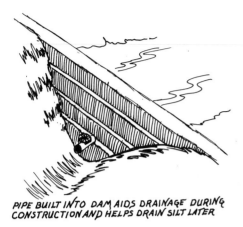

PIPE BUILT INTO DAM AIDS DRAINAGE DURING
CONSTRUCTION AND HELPS DRAIN SILT LATER

Figure 15-7. A drain pipe is handy at the base of the dam during construction to keep water away from the mortar, and later for use in draining the pond to clean out sill.

FOOTING

In pouring the footing, don't worry about still water in the ditch. Flowing water should be carried on downstream in a pipe or flume over your footing (Fig. 15-7), but the concrete will set up even under water, as long as it's contained. Remember how the water rises to the top of cement mixed too wet? The mix will settle, solidify, and cure as long as moving water is kept away from it.

You can move the pipe or flume around as you lay stone for the dam itself. If you use a pipe, you can leave it in one spot and incorporate it for use as a drain later. If you don't leave the pipe in, you'll need to keep the water pumped or shiphoned from upstream to downstream while your work sets up, which requires some round-the-clock supervision.

DIMENSIONS

Make the dam proportionately thicker than you would a wall. I like a 1-foot-thick base for a 2-foot-high dam, or a 2-foot base for a 4-foot dam. Since I always narrow the dam at the top to as little as 6 inches thick, I make the footing only as thick as the base—not double that, as I do for a wall. So a 3-foot-high stone dam would have an 18-inch-thick footing at least 6 inches deep, topped by an 18-inch dam narrowing to 6 inches at the top. Pressure is greatest at the bottom, so the dam is thicker here. But it's not downward pressure so much (as in a foundation) but side pressure from the water. See Fig. 15-8.

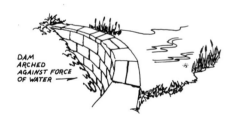

DAM
ARCHED
AGAINST
FORCE
OF WATER ➝

Figure 15-6. A stone dam can be arched against the water for strength or be buttressed on the downstream side.

BRACING

If yours is a swift stream that drops sharply, arch your dam against the force (Fig. 15-6). The structure is the same as for a vertical arch, keystone and all. This one is thicker at the base and may taper from the back, front, or both—or it may not narrow at the top at all, if you want it wide enough for a walkway there.

Another form of bracing is the downstream buttress, set on an extension of the footing. A drawback is the tendency of overflow water to undermine the buttress, making its weight a detriment instead of a brace. It will brace well if the footing is deep enough and the stream bottom is lined with stones.

The spillway of your dam can be no more than the water coming over the top. It's a good idea to thicken the base of the dam downstream to lessen undercutting by the falling water (Fig. 15-9). If you arrange for the overflow to go another route, remember to line it with stone. The Morah Mill dam overflow on Spring River near Carthage, Missouri, is lined with stones lapped like shingles to hold the soil. Very effective (Fig. 15-5).

Figure 15-10. Drystone work, plastered on the upstream side, formed the original dam at Jolly Mill. Repair work of mortared stone at left was added as the stream began to cut a new channel around the end of the dam, which it eventually succeeded in doing.

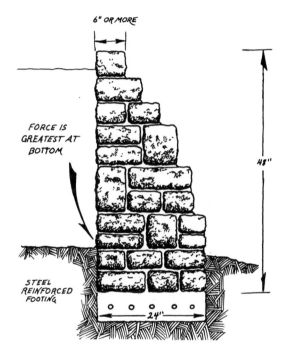

6" OR MORE

FORCE IS GREATEST AT BOTTOM

48"

STEEL REINFORCED FOOTING

24"

Figure 15-8. The dam can be thin at the top, where pressure is less, cutting down on the quantity of stone needed.

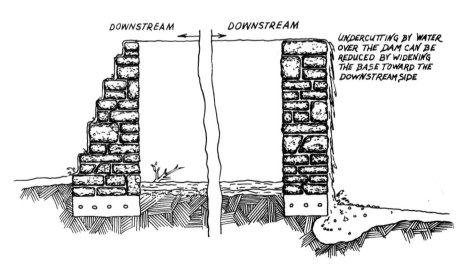

DOWNSTREAM   DOWNSTREAM

UNDERCUTTING BY WATER OVER THE DAM CAN BE REDUCED BY WIDENING THE BASE TOWARD THE DOWNSTREAM SIDE

Figure 15-9. A vertical stone dam invites overflow water to eat back under it; if stepped, the water's force is broken and is directed outward.

KEEP IT UP

A dam needs maintenance. I've seen old mill dams beautifully intact, with the stream running free around the end through a new channel (Fig. 15-10). And I've seen small leaks grow until the whole dam gives way. Overflow water undercutting the structure on the downstream side is another hazard. I've seen dams tilted and sunk almost flat from this.

The pond will fill in with silt, sand, gravel, and other solids as time passes. It's a natural action when moving water becomes still. A pipe at the bottom of the dam will let you drain and flush the pond if you want, or you may pump it dry and dig it out. For power generation, you're probably going to take water from the top anyway, so filling it doesn't really matter. It does matter if you need a reserve capacity, as when you would draw down the pond level from a low outlet for sustained power over a period of time.

HARNESSING THE ENERGY

Once built, let's say you do plan to take power from the falling water. I've studied waterwheel design in mill restoration work, and there are three basic kinds. The overshot wheel (Fig. 15-14) is most efficient, with watertight buckets that fill at the top, weight the wheel, and dump at the bottom. The breast wheel (Fig. 15-12) fills its buckets partway up and turns against a formed chute, or breast. The undershot wheel (Fig. 15-13) is basically a paddle wheel down into the moving water, which may be channeled closely.

The overshot requires a drop higher than the wheel, but less flow than the others, since practically all the water is used. The breast wheel will inevitably waste some water around the wheel in spite of the close-fitting chute, but it requires less height. The undershot, which is least efficient, can utilize very little drop but must have significantly more flow for effectiveness. This wheel can be improved with curved paddles open at the back (the Poncelet wheel) to generate more motion from the force of the water.

TURBINE

The water turbine (Fig. 15-11) was developed a long time ago (around 1840) as an improvement over the wheel. It is useful in applications where there is lots of flow and little fall, so a low dam on a river was often built. The turbine housing and rotor work together to extract more force from the falling water than a wheel can. Steam, hydraulic, and gas turbines were developed from this basic principle. The torque converter in an automobile transmission had its genesis in the water mill turbine.

If you have dreams of becoming self-sufficient via water power generation, my advice is to scale your power requirements to the absolute minimum. Most of us are so spoiled by overuse of power that to duplicate it ourselves would require a river each, plus a big portion of our lives spent learning the necessary technology, plus more years converting it to our uses.

Getting a 12-volt light bulb to flicker or operating a piston pump to water a garden is a bit easier, but we soon want to go on to refrigeration, stereo, well pump, and other gadgetry. Of the many folks I know who've gone back to the earth to live, most have either not gone all that far or have returned after short stays.

Let me hasten to say that I deplore the monthly utility bill as much as anyone. And let me further say that I've tried several alternative energy methods and sources. Some of them worked. It becomes a simple matter of what you want to spend your days doing and whether you will be content with bare subsistence as time goes on.

But we'll always be fascinated by the prospect of altering natural forces like moving water, and there have certainly been benefits from it. For my part, I prefer the less spectacular ones—a lazy gristmill creaking, instead of Hoover Dam.

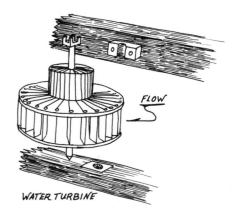

WATER TURBINE

Figure 15-11. The water turbine is more efficient than a waterwheel. It consists of pitched blades inside a housing (not shown) and is best used with heavy flow and can be effective with little stream fall.

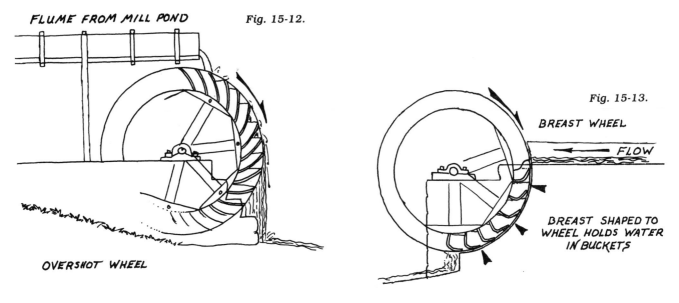

FLUME FROM MILL POND   Fig. 15-12.

OVERSHOT WHEEL

Fig. 15-13.

BREAST WHEEL

FLOW

BREAST SHAPED TO WHEEL HOLDS WATER IN BUCKETS

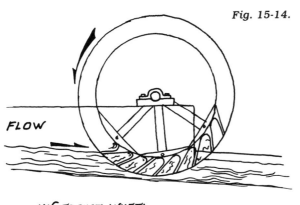

Fig. 15-14.

FLOW

UNDERSHOT WHEEL

Figures 15-12—15-14. The three principal types of waterwheel. Each is best suited for a particular streambed condition.

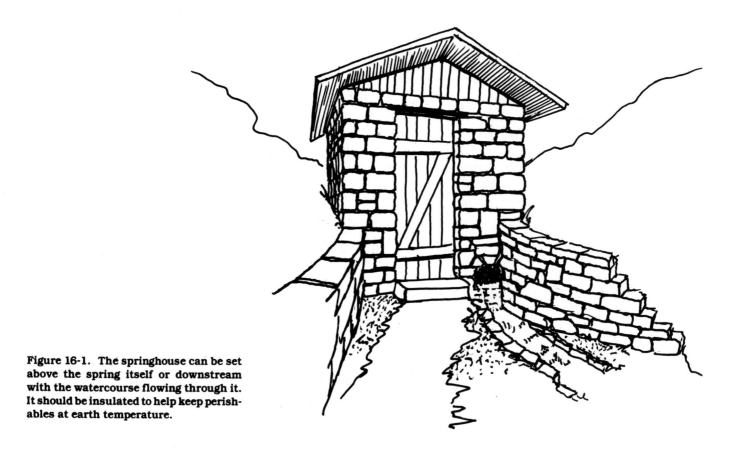

Figure 16-1. The springhouse can be set above the spring itself or downstream with the watercourse flowing through it. It should be insulated to help keep perishables at earth temperature.

SPRINGHOUSE, WELL HOUSE

THE SPRINGHOUSE was a vital rural structure before refrigeration. Milk would spoil in a day without cooling, eggs and butter soon after. The chill of 56-degree earth-temperature water surrounding earthenware crocks and jugs allowed housewives a little flexibility in using up perishables.

Today the function of the springhouse is exactly the same, in those areas where refrigeration is either impossible, too expensive, or just not your choice. A stone structure traditionally, the springhouse was built either over the spring or right below it, to allow use of the water at its coldest (Fig. 16-1). It functions a little like a root cellar, being a short-term storage place. With the cold water right against the containers, however, cooling is faster.

Of course, first you need a spring, and while most of these beautifully natural fountains have become polluted beyond consumption of the water, they can still serve to cool things (even a dirty refrigerator can work). A brisk flow of water is better, but a mere trickle will keep pools of water cool.

During my youth in central Arkansas, we often cooled things in our spring and water supply, which had barely a ¾-inch pipe flow. We had no springhouse, but we had built a submerged box of concrete brick to keep out the constantly flowing sand. Into this box went containers of perishables; out came drinking water. We were later to use a hydraulic ram of my father's design and construction, and still later a piston pump.

But ours wasn't a typical case. The spring was some 300 yards off through the woods, and we didn't dare trust much stuff to the wildlife. We also used the old practice of lowering such things as jugs of milk in a bucket to hang in our well. The water wasn't good in any of the several wells we dug, but again, cool was cool.

WELL HOUSE

A modern structure similar to the springhouse is the well house, sheltering pump and often pressure tank, and keeping them from freezing. Both structures house running water—one to keep heat in, one to keep it out. Both can be quite small, as little as 4 by 6 feet, although you may want more room.

Let's look at a 6x8-foot size, which will let you move around a bit inside. I recall one that size on a grown-up tangle of homestead in Nelson County, Virginia, a neat example located below the spring,

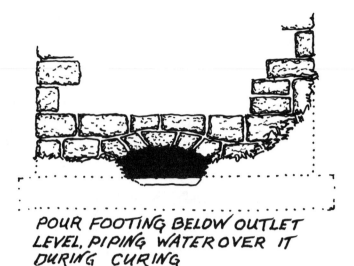

Figure 16-2. The springhouse should be set on a slab with the water outlet above, large enough for increased flow during wet weather.

POUR FOOTING BELOW OUTLET LEVEL, PIPING WATER OVER IT DURING CURING

with the runoff through it. The whole thing was shaded by gnarled, ancient Jonathan apple trees, and it happened we were there in Indian summer. The apples and the spring water were delightfully crisp. Another that same size was on the banks of the Buffalo River in Arkansas. This one was of hewn heart-cedar logs—no telling how old—which had just begun to decay when I first saw the springhouse in 1972. The spring rose right up, in this one, and ran out under a wall in a profusion of watercress.

It's a good idea to dig out your spring first and rock it up with squarish drystone so the water can come through nicely to fill pools of varying depth. You could do this after you build the house, or you could even let part of the footing and wall contain the spring. The well, of course, will have to be drilled or dug beforehand, since this operation takes lots of space.

STOP HEAT GAIN

Since you're dealing with heat here, mortar your stone and pour a good footing (Fig. 16-2). Build as you would any structure, omitting windows that would transmit heat. You can double- or triple-glaze a window if you really want one, remembering to keep the layers of glass ¾ inch or less apart, so as not to allow circulation of the dead air between.

Insulation is necessary here, particularly overhead. You could heap earth up around the outside of either well house or springhouse and not insulate the walls, but the roof would still require it. And since you're dealing with moisture here, choose waterproof insulation such as Styrofoam or urea-formaldehyde foam. Remember that wet fiber insulation is no insulation.

The foam sheets can be nailed to the roof with wide-head roofing nails, if you use enough of them, or glued with a special adhesive. They can be nailed to the masonry walls with masonry nails if you use a wide washer of some kind (heavy cardboard will do) under the head. It makes more sense to nail furring strips to the wall and attach the foam boards to them.

A spring is just about always down in at least a little hollow, and it's relatively simple to heap dirt up around the springhouse to maintain earth temperature. If you have trees overhanging the spring, you probably won't want to do this—and neither would I—so insulate. A well can be drilled anywhere that's accessible, so the dirt treatment, called berm-type building, may have to be more contrived there.

Two or 3 inches of foam board will suffice for the walls (door, too), with 4 inches in the roof. For so small a structure the roof itself can be no more than 2x4s based on plates bolted to the tops of the stone walls. Just leave the doorway open to the top if you like, and span it with 2x4s or a 4x4-inch lintel. On this small structure, the walls need not be joined overhead for stability.

In the case of the well house, you want it tight all around. The springhouse must have a way for the water to get out, so leave a screened opening to discourage critters under part of the downstream walls, preferably over the continuous reinforced footing. Pipe the moving water over the footing when you pour it, so it won't wash out. Remember that concrete will cure beneath still water; just don't let the water get flowing.

If your spring tends to run high after a rain, which most wet-weather ones do, leave enough room for the maximum flow or you'll flood the springhouse. If there's no flow in the dry months, the springhouse won't do much good, since that's when you'll need the cooling. A root cellar will do as well, and it's drier.

You could divert water from a stream through a buried pipe and create your own spring if you really wanted to. The water would cool to earth temperature as it flowed, and emerge cold. If you screened the intake in the stream and could cope with freezing in winter (flexible plastic pipe seldom bursts with freezing), you could handle it.

But that's doing it the hard way. If your wilderness retreat is like most, you'll be covered with building jobs without creating more. Or if your projects are confined to the suburbs, you probably won't have the space.

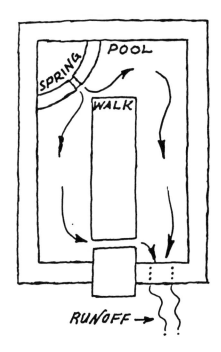

Figure 16-3. This floor plan for a springhouse shows a walkway with shallow pools on each side fed by the spring within the structure. Water should flow freely to stay cold.

DESIGN

The layout for a springhouse can be whatever you like. I wall up the spring itself (Fig. 16-5), so I can dip a bucket into the deep water. Then I channel the overflow into one or more shallow, rock-bottom pools to set the crockery in. You want cold water to come up as high as possible without covering or floating containers. It's a good idea to have a stepped bottom here for varying depth.

One pool is fine if you can reach everything; using two, with a dry walkway between (Fig. 16-3), puts things within easier reach. Channel the runoff to one side of the door so you don't have to wade in.

Build your well house with a hinged roof or a trapdoor that can be opened. Sooner or later you'll have to pull the pipe up for repairs, or the whole pump if it's submersible. If yours is no more than a well box, just leave the roof so it can be lifted off. But you will probably want room to move around in there, so give yourself more space. A surface pump always needs a new belt or a bit of oil. And you can put a faucet in there so it won't freeze.

CONVERTED SPRINGHOUSE

Easily the most impressive springhouse I know of is one owned by friends of ours near Purcellville, Virginia, that has been remodeled into a guest house. The water table has lowered or the stream has been diverted, or both, and now this small but massive stone structure has two stories and a sleeping loft that are quite dry. The woodwork, a wonder of space-saving, is heavy and finely done. And the thick stone walls have been treated with a craftsman's respect.

This springhouse is visually still just that from the outside and is a very good example of the conversion of a once-useful structure

Figure 16-4. This Missouri springhouse is of cut limestone, with an upper entrance and steps down inside.

into a different but again-useful one without sacrificing any of its charms. It is a fitting complement to the restored main log house.

You won't have much choice in the location of your springhouse unless you do divert the water. But wherever you put it, the moisture will encourage growth of moss and visual aging that will blend it to the surroundings better than just about any other building. Plant mint and maybe watercress along and in the runoff stream for kitchen use and as a further bit of landscaping. You can do some nice things with little stone bridges across the stream to blend with the springhouse, too. And if you don't have the trees at the spring, plant some to help shade the whole area. It'll be a cool place all around.

You can start an oasis at the well house, too, by having a faucet there to make it easier to keep things green. Choose your well site with some forethought as to how the well will complement your main house and the total layout you're working with. Fast-growing trees such as mimosa and mulberry will make it less barren sooner, and the well house, too, can become a nice focal point in your landscaping.

Figure 16-5. This nicely walled-up spring has a reservoir pool inside. It's in a steep valley on the Gloucester Forge property in the Blue Ridge.

Figure 17-1. A stone house lends itself to arched windows. These have keystones, braced with angle iron in the upper Palladian arch.

STONE HOUSE

MY OWN EXPERIENCE with stone houses began in the 1940s when my father, older brother, and I built a massive little farmhouse in central Arkansas. The walls were 16 inches thick, the doors and windows were arched, and the fireplace was a veritable cave.

We picked stone from all over the 40 acres surrounding the site, sledding it to the hilltop on a series of stoneboats behind a spirited, long-legged mare. My memory is dim, but we must have hauled many hundreds of loads out of fields, woods and grown-up thickets.

This particular house was built with wooden forms for concrete on the inside. A layer of random stone, laid up as we poured and filled the form, was used as the outside surface. We'd pour a mixer-load of concrete, then toss in odd-shaped rocks to help fill. Later we pointed up, or filled in the cracks between the random face rocks from outside, with cement.

Building went on for years, as I finished grade school and went on to high school. Electric power came to our part of rural Arkansas about then, and the new house was to have electricity. My father designed a series of heating pipes for the floors to carry water heated in a coil from the chimney.

We were able to replace our hydraulic ram with a water pump, which didn't clog with sand from the spring or freeze up in winter. Truman was President, and I remember my civics teacher assuring us that Stalin would eventually die and the world would be safe from Russia.

And the walls of our house grew. Today I can visit the place and trace where different batches of concrete were poured, showing that sand or gravel came from one or another small creekbed nearby.

My parents have never accustomed themselves to any degree of luxurious living, and I now realize that cottage was Spartan in the extreme. The log house I live in with my wife and daughters is filled with far more conveniences and comforts. But the fascination with stone in building had begun, and it has led me to explore lots of applications for the material.

Of course the ultimate challenge is a dwelling house—not the cold, damp peasant hut of my Celtic ancestors of the gloomy Gothic-novel manors of the moors, but a livable house—warm, dry, well-lighted, efficient, and so very durable.

PROS AND CONS

First you must remember that stone has several major

Figures 17-2—17-5. (Above) Early stone house in East Tennessee. Masons were often brought in from the older states by well-to-do planters to build in this region around 1800. (Left) The stone cottage wing at Greystone, of six-inch sandstone with inner studwall. (Upper right) Relatively modern stone house and wall south of Fayetteville, Arkansas, of Ozark Mountain sandstone. (Lower right) Store building in Osage, Arkansas. Arches are cut stone, walls rough ledge pattern.

shortcomings you will have to overcome. As we said at the beginning of this book, it is heavy; its insulation properties are almost nonexistent; it sweats. It is probably the most expensive material, in terms of time and labor, you can find to build with. And it takes one mountain of rocks to build a house.

Now that we have these negatives noted, let's see how you can overcome them. First, plan massive footings for the weight, and double walls or inner walls, with insulation and moisture barriers between, to take care of heat loss and dampness. And just forget about your investment in time and labor. Charge it off as therapy or make it your road to physical fitness. (After all, this is your contribution to the good architecture of the world, and you can suffer a little for your art.)

You'll still need lots of rocks, but you'll find them. You will develop a roving eye that picks out the telltale flash of sandstone among the roadside scrub. You will return from trips with specimens in the trunk of your car among the sales reports. You will acquire your own midden of material that will grow from secret sources.

And you will not—will *not*—rush building your stone house. It is to be an exercise in patience and quality craftsmanship. Remember that the mistakes you make in stone are damn permanent, so do it right.

DESIGN

Let's say yours is to be, first of all, a simple rectangle with a ridge running the long way. You can add to it later in any of several ways

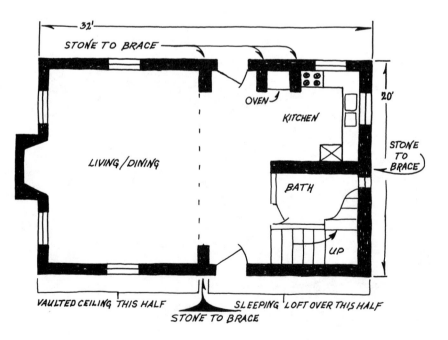

Figure 17-6. Stone walls intersecting the main walls brace where needed and can be incorporated as part of the living function. The fireplace braces one wall, the stone bathroom another. The oven can be set into a stone bracing wall, and the front wall can have either an interior entry wall or partial wall, or a stone porch with some sort of wall.

for space and convenience. But let's start with a 20x32-foot house with a sleeping loft over half of it (Fig. 17-6). Tuck your kitchen and bath into the end opposite the fireplace, under the loft, and use one corner for the stairs. You'll still have enough room for living and dining room in the unpartitioned fireplace end. An interior stone wall for the bathroom can brace one end of the house, the chimney the other. A partial wall at the back could incorporate an oven in the kitchen and brace this wall. An entryway inside or a stone porch in front could do the same for the remaining wall.

We're looking at the business of designing a house just backward here, but we're doing it for a reason. You'd ordinarily and correctly design from the inside out, creating work spaces and living spaces in accordance with your needs. The shape of the house would grow outward from these needs, assuming the appearance thus dictated, which would still fit the site. This blending of house with surroundings while fitting living needs is what dwelling-house design is all about.

But here I want to stress the structural requirements of building with stone, so we'll use this simplified design. By no means would I want you to adjust your own needs to my ideas or anyone else's. That's what those look-alike designs syndicated through newspapers do. (Does anybody ever actually build one of those, or are they collected to yellow on some shelf while he who clipped them languishes in a cramped apartment?)

GETTING STARTED

Let's go ahead. Dig a footing twice wall thickness to below frost line to carry the weight of your walls. Pour a footing about 12 inches deep, with four ½-inch reinforcing rods in it. Bring the walls to the level of the floor, which may be a concrete slab or wood on joists. If it's to be a slab, you pour it on packed fill, with insulation and vapor barrier underneath, out over at least part of the wall thickness (Fig. 17-7). Reinforce the slab with welded wire mesh or, to save money, use recycled wire fencing. Lay it flat on a sheet of black plastic over the packed floor area. When the 4 inches or so of concrete is poured and spread out, hook the wire and pull it up into the concrete to about the center. You'll use a screed, which is a board up on edge, to level the slab; then finish with the trowel.

There's a lot to concrete work that has nothing at all to do with building with stone. I'd suggest that you give a lot of thought to having the floor done by a professional contractor. Nothing is worse than a wavy floor.

Crushed stone or gravel 4" deep is best here, with the plastic over it or underneath.

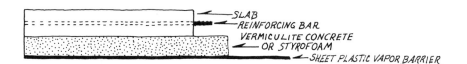

Figure 17-7. A concrete slab floor should have a vapor barrier and insulation under it to cut downward heat loss.

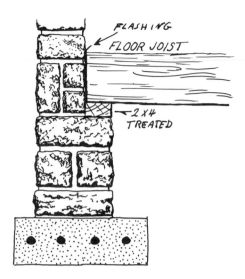

FLASHING
FLOOR JOIST
2x4
TREATED

Figure 17-8. Floor joists for a wooden floor are best set on a ledge in the stone. A stone house wall footing should be heavily reinforced.

The 2x4 set on the foundation ledge for the joist ends to rest on should be pressure-treated, and a pressure-treated band is recommended at the end of the joists as both a safeguard against decay and a bar to termites. Metal flashing can also be used in both these locations for the same purposes.

If you do it yourself, lay a couple of inches of industrial Styrofoam over the vapor barrier for insulation, or pour a sub-slab of 4 inches of vermiculite-mixed concrete, with the reinforced slab over this. Heat loss is mostly through the ceiling, but you lose a lot downward, too.

SUPPORT THE FLOOR

If the floor is to be joisted, you'll want to build in a ledge inside each wall to set the joists on (Fig. 17-8). A 4-inch ledge is enough. I've seen wooden blocks set into the wall for the joists to be spiked to, but a solid ledge is stronger. This means starting the wall 4 inches thicker than it will be above the floor. A simple way to get the ledge level is to set a 2x4 flat at the right height, held at two or three points, then build up to it.

Sometimes I leave floor joists and flooring till after the roof is on, to protect them from the weather. Stone construction is apt to take a long time, so if you put these in now, cover them to keep them dry. Midway of their 20-foot length, you'll need to support the joists with a sleeper, supported in turn by stone or concrete piers (Fig. 17-10). I use two shorter lengths for joists, lapping at the center over the sleeper. Long timbers are harder to find and generally cost more per foot.

Insulate the floor, which means a wire mesh, slats, or solid plywood or fiberboard under the joists to hold it up. I like 6 inches of fiberglass or its equivalent in the floor. (When choosing insulation, you should know that listed R values are theoretical and that just a bit of moisture, dust, or compaction can cut real effectiveness in half.) Leave vents in the walls below the floor for air circulation or you will have moisture, which will eventually rot the wood (Fig. 17-9).

Figure 17-9. If the floor is wood, insulate under and provide vents for air circulation to reduce moisture.

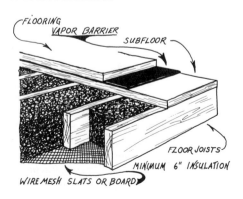

FLOORING
VAPOR BARRIER
SUBFLOOR
FLOOR JOISTS
MINIMUM 6" INSULATION
WIRE MESH SLATS OR BOARD

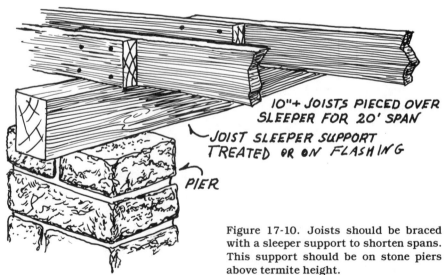

10"+ JOISTS PIECED OVER SLEEPER FOR 20' SPAN
JOIST SLEEPER SUPPORT TREATED OR ON FLASHING
PIER

Figure 17-10. Joists should be braced with a sleeper support to shorten spans. This support should be on stone piers above termite height.

Lay the floor in the conventional manner, with subfloor of boards or plywood. I use rough-sawn lumber here. Your finished floor can wait till partitions are in.

WALLS

Go ahead with the walls, either anchoring studs to the inside on a sill over the subfloor for an inner wall or building two stone walls with insulation and vapor barrier between (Fig. 17-11). I like a stone interior; but it gets tiresome visually, so I'd suggest a combination, with at least the entire wall at the fireplace end a double stone wall. Other walls could be studding covered inside with paneling or dry wall.

Frame doors and windows with subfacings anchored to the stone as you go up. I set bolts into the rockwork with the nuts countersunk into the subfacing boards so I can tighten them up later, as discussed in Chapter Nine. Be sure to allow for the thickness of the finish facings here.

You'll build your fireplace right into the wall as you go up rather than later, as with a log or frame house. You will have poured the chimney slab along with the foundation footing, and now above floor level you'll form the fireplace opening as you build. In a stone house, I like the fireplace flush with the inside wall so that it appears as an integral part of the wall, not a separate structure.

Most builders terminate the masonry walls above windows and doors so there's no need to span them. A good arch, flat keystone span, or lintel looks more substantial; besides, it's a testimony to your craft. We went into detail on these spans in Chapter Eight, so use those principles here.

CEILING JOINTS

If you plan a knee wall above the ceiling for more headroom upstairs—and I advise it—you'll do better to build in the ceiling joists than leave another ledge. If you leave another 4 inches for the joist ends to rest on, that cuts your wall thickness. And if you've made the entire wall thicker to allow for this, you've got a lot more wall than you need.

We didn't build in the floor joists, because that tends to trap moisture down near the earth and rot them. Up here things stay drier. You don't go all the way through with the joist ends. If yours is a double stone wall, the inside one will carry the joist ends nicely. If it's to have a stud wall inside, that can support the joists (Fig. 17-12).

Of course, if there's to be no knee wall upstairs, the joists go right across to rest on the wall plate, tied to the rafters to form the roof trusses. But since you'll have lots more room with 3 feet or so of knee wall, let's do it. Check local codes, if any, for minimum height here.

If you have a knee wall, there needn't be any ceiling joists across the open vaulted ceiling part of the house since you'll need another way to stop lateral wall thrust (which we'll talk about later). But you may want one or two for appearance. If you go ahead and build them

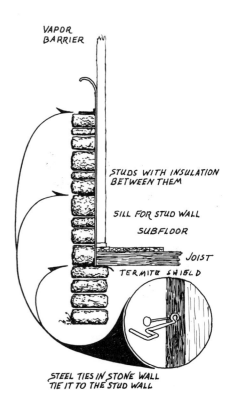

VAPOR BARRIER

STUDS WITH INSULATION BETWEEN THEM

SILL FOR STUD WALL

SUBFLOOR

JOIST

TERMITE SHIELD

STEEL TIES IN STONE WALL
TIE IT TO THE STUD WALL

Figure 17-11. If an inner wall is built using studs with insulation between, anchor them to the stone with metal ties. Use a vapor barrier on the living side of the insulation.

A rule of thumb for joist size is one inch in height for every two feet spanned, or an eight-inch joist (such as a 6x8) for a 16' span, or a ten-inch joist for a 20' span. Where applicable, building codes should be consulted and followed. Joist spacing also depends on the strength and thickness of the flooring that is to go overhead. Two-inch tongue-in-groove flooring allows greater spacing than the allowable one-inch flooring.

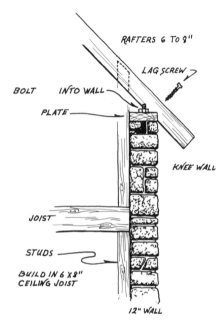

Figures 17-12 and 17-13. With a double stone wall, insulated between, the ceiling joists can be supported by the inner wall. They can be set on the studwall if that construction is used.

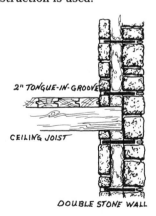

in, you can floor the entire loft later if you choose. Open ceilings are hard for some people to live with, since heat goes up there and stays.

Those joists that support the ceiling/loft floor should be a maximum of 4 feet apart. I like at least a 6 x 8-inch dimension for the joists themselves. And the ceiling should be 2-inch tongue-in-groove lumber to help span the distance. Lay this on top of the joists and leave them exposed from below. See Fig. 17-13.

ROOF SUPPORT

Set bolts into the top of the stone walls for the plates, which are timbers that provide support for the rafters. These can be 2 inches thick or more. And anchor the rafters to the plates with boils or lag screws, so the roof won't lift off in a windstorm.

Now, with the rafters in place you need a very important pair of braces in each roof slope. They should run from each corner of the house up to the peak at or near the center, to carry the weight of the roof in a triangulated structure to avoid outward thrust on the walls.

In other words, with a knee wall upstairs, there's no way the joists, even though they run front to back, can hold the tops of the walls in, and the roof must bear straight down only, not outward. These angle braces tie everything up there together so the roof can sit on the walls without shoving them out. The braces also take any thrust from the gable ends of the roof. See Fig. 17-14.

Many builders brace the rafters against outward push with just a cross girt above head height, leaving the lower part of the rafters to spring outward. The effect of this is shown in the drawings in Chapter Seven. With stone, you can't have any outward thrust, so don't count on this high brace. I'd brace the ceiling joists with either king posts down from the peak or pairs of queen posts (Fig. 17-15). Without them, the 20-foot span will tremble underfoot no matter how heavy the joists are. And they can be a problem. King posts effectively cut your loft in two, and you may not want that with just 20 feet total depth. Queen posts place the uprights out toward the knee walls, leaving a path down the center.

OTHER BRACING

The alternative is post supports from below, but that cuts up your area down there. This is why most modern buildings have a wall down the center of the house no matter what. On today's pancake houses, the wall braces both the ceilings joists and the low peak of the roof. With a steeper pitch of, say, 45 degrees, you get all that upstairs space and snow melts or slides off sooner. (And if you've faced the ridge to the south, you can do a good thing with solar heat on a steep roof.)

With our design, we can do a little of both kinds of bracing to achieve our ends. The bathroom/kitchen wall can brace from below for about half the length of the loft, or two joists. The third can be king or queen post braced from above, or with a lone post from

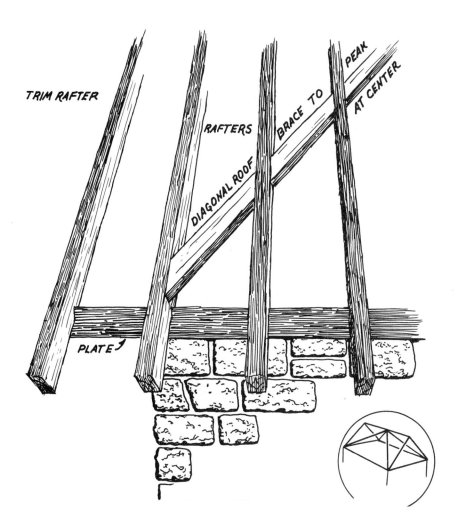

TRIM RAFTER

RAFTERS

DIAGONAL ROOF BRACE TO PEAK AT CENTER

PLATE

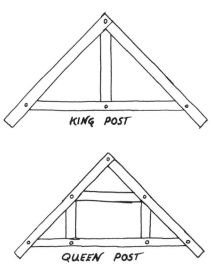

Figure 17-14. For any building with some wall above the ceiling joists, this diagonal rafter brace will take roof weight out to the corners where the end walls can carry it. This keeps the roof from sagging and the weight from pushing out on the side walls.

KING POST

QUEEN POST

Figure 17-15. The queen post utilizes two uprights to provide space between; the king post one, splitting the upstairs space. Both support the ceiling joist against sagging.

below. Either way is a bit of a bother, but the post, if from below, doesn't have to be in the center of the joist. Play around with it. The last joist, being at the end of the loft, can have either king or queen post bracing down from the top, since that's as far as you'll go up there. You'll want a railing, too.

Your roof can box in the rafters with insulation between, or be a double affair on top, leaving the rafters as exposed beams inside. Insulate heavily here—at the very least, 6 inches of fiberglass—because heat goes up and out. This design, or any design with a vaulted ceiling, means that a lot of the heat will stay around up there, but you can exhaust it at the peak in summer with an attic fan. In winter you can circulate it with a blower, or just let it stay up there and maybe sleep raw.

LET LIGHT IN

Any house with a loft will be dark, because you have places for windows only at the gable ends. An alternative is a skylight, but I have seen few that do not leak in time. I prefer dormer windows, and this design's 32-foot length would allow two small ones front and back for more light. I'd say 3-foot-wide structures with about 24-inch windows in them would be proportionate.

If you want a balcony, you can put a flat top on your porch, front or back, and make the dormer windows French, so they let you outside.

UTILITIES

As for plumbing and wiring in a stone house, you must plan ahead. The stud wall inside makes it simple, as in any ticky-tacky. If you've built two stone walls, you'll need to do things with pipes and wires on the inward side of the insulation as you build.

And since it will be a major demolition job to get at a burst pipe, be sure to have outlets at low places so that all water can be drained if the house is left unheated in winter. Heat tape is nice, too, while you're gone.

Polybutylene pipe is flexible, and will withstand freezing. We use it almost exclusively for both hot and cold water in new construction and restoration work.

PLAN CAREFULLY

The fascination of building your own dwelling with the stone from your woods may be strong. Certainly stone is a fitting and natural material, satisfying the basic craving for shelter and protection deep in each of us. And stone from the site does more to blend a house with the landscape than anything else you can do.

But be aware that if a wall proves to be in the wrong place, you're just about going to have to live with it; it won't come out as easily as a stud wall. And knocking out a doorway to add more room is a major task. And of course you must realize that you will be a-building for many months on even a small house, so don't deadline yourself into a corner.

There is a great deal more to building a dwelling house of any kind than we can cover here, and most designs are more involved than this one. Before you attempt a stone house, I'd say you should have built at least one house out of wood, and just about everything else you can think of out of stone.

By that time you'll know more what you're up against. And you'll be either hard to talk into building a stone house or hard to talk out of it.

Figures 17-16 and 17-17. (Above) The basement kitchen at Page Meadows, showing post-and-beam with stone fill, triple-wall construction. (Left) This corner in our house is a study in textures: The stone fill with heartpine beamwork, some hewn, some planed and oiled. The logs are hewn, with masonry mortar chinking. Stairs are of 3-inch thick heartpine.

Figure 18-1. Pebble barn near Harrison, Arkansas, with a pile of the stone it's built of—chunks of chert picked out of the fields. This barn was built of formed and poured concrete, with the stones filling and facing the walls.

CHAPTER EIGHTEEN

STONE BARN

STONE IS probably the best material you could find for a barn. It's much better for a barn than for a dwelling house. You can shut out drafts with a tight mortared wall or hold against a cut hillside for earth temperature. You can have a snug, solid building with no need for inner walls, insulation, vapor barriers, or a floor. The very body heat given off by the animals will keep temperatures—especially in a barn dug into a hill—quite tolerable.

Pennsylvania is of course the country for barns, and the best stone barns I've seen are there. Hillside barns, with one level cut back into the earth so you come in above it on the uphill side. Barns big enough to dwarf the houses and to stand as proof of the farmer's prosperity, industry, and expertise. Beautiful barns, with their wooden gables and upper stories painted the very red you want a barn to be, sometimes with hex signs in white or yellow or blue, and small windows trimmed in the same colors.

OTHER BARNS

In my country, the barn was unfortunately an afterthought. The hill man often had no more than a shed on cedar poles set into the ground, open on one side, with a roof of shingles or tin. West and north of the Ozarks where I live, the prairies flatten out like ironed wrinkles and the barns begin—Missouri barns, without the gambrel roof you find east, barns that look for all the world like saltbox houses, with that catslide roof down over outside stalls or a machinery shed along one side. Sometimes the roof angle breaks to house sheds on both sides, like a mother hen spreading her wings over her chicks.

These barns are rarely stone, except for some pebble ones with small rounded creekbed stones or irregular chunks from the fields stacked into the forms to face concrete walls when they were poured. When it was cheaper than it is now, concrete made a good barn, though not a good-looking barn by itself.

One of my favorite barns is in East Swanzey, New Hampshire, built, I understand, before the Revolution. A plain barn this, with no fanciful designs. A working barn, not connected to the house as many are in that country, this one rises from a stone story set into a slope. And those stones! Quarried granite slabs and beams 10 and 12 feet long laid dry to hold out the soil uphill and base the barn above (Fig. 18-2).

Figure 18-2. Quarried granite stones dry-laid to form the first story of the barn in East Swanzey. Even the fenceposts on this farm were cut from granite.

Its beams are hewn with a skill I do not often find in barns. Trusses, plates, rafters of awesome length, true in dimension, straight, aged brown with a glow rubbed by livestock, by hay, by the feel of hands. Rafters soar up to a half-notched and pegged peak, with wide, whipsawn slatting, rough-edged, showing shakes from the underside.

This is a commonplace barn, which I suppose is why I like it. No showpiece—you'd pass it without its presence registering. Reroofed countless times, upper-level wall boards replaced, weathered, replaced again. Bearing the forged hinge pintles of long-ago doors set into worn upright beams, replaced with sliding doors now nailed shut. Its present owners have begun wedging loose stones, bracing sagging beams. With care it should easily last another couple of hundred years.

BLUFF BARN

Perhaps the most unique barn I know of anywhere is a stone barn of sorts on the Buffalo River in Arkansas. Actually it consists only of a pen of logs roughly notched at the corners. You see, it's set far back under an overhanging bluff, dry in all seasons. An old military road crossed the river here, and records indicate that the bluff was used for barn space for nearly 150 years, and probably by the Indians of the region before that. Wagons, hay, feed, fence posts—everything you'd expect to find in a barn is stored here, although with increased river traffic the owners have stopped storing portable farm tools.

The overhang is some 40 feet, running along some distance from the present river course. In times past, it's been the scene of picnics, revivals, folk festivals, and square dances, as well as military encampments. It could actually house twenty barns.

A barn is the measure of how well you farm, of how well you care for your assorted critters, from cows to tractor. We're talking simple shelter here, and like all good construction, it should be as permanent as you can build it. To me that means stone, of course.

SIZE IMPORTANT

A barn is almost by necessity a big building, to house hay in sufficient quantities, as well as livestock and your machinery, so that means a lot of stone. I'd say build a stone barn if you're covered up with rocks on your place, but not otherwise. Acquiring stone for a barbecue pit is one thing; moving a mountain for a 60-foot barn quite another.

In estimating the size of your stone barn, proceed on the principle that you can't have too much room. I deplore this attitude when applied to dwelling houses, since a creative use of well-designed smaller space makes for better architecture. But a barn will be used for things you'd never anticipate when planning it: things like firewood, and the workshop you'll never build, and the dry-rotted sailboat you bought on impulse that you'll restore next year. And all the stuff you've left outside till now. (You'll be able to *find* it all, in the barn.)

A barn is essentially an enclosure for storing hay and feed above, with stalls, stanchions, and stables below. If we settle on a 40x60-foot size, with just one or perhaps two levels of stone, the job approaches realistic proportions. That's 200 feet of wall, of course, but there will be doorways on the downhill side below, on the uphill side above, and two huge openings for the drive-through—plus a few windows. That's still a lot of rock. Overhead you'll have a beamed and raftered framework that's mostly roof, which is no small chore in itself.

BIT BY BIT

My brother John is solving barn construction by building in sections. He began with one side of his proposed structure, maybe only half the length, so he had a sixth of the eventual total at first. Roofed it with a shed roof that will eventually join more roof over the open breezeway down the center. He has minimal loft space above the stalls. The next unit is to be the other side, set the width of the breezeway apart from the first. Then a loft will join the two. The whole thing can be extended as his need for space grows.

You could easily do this, too, remembering to leave a stepped end for a better joint if you plan to join the stone wall. I'd say tackle the entire thing, since you can leave stonework out in the weather indefinitely. When you're ready for the wood part, plan a mammoth barn raising to get it up and covered before it can rot down.

DIG IN

If you set your barn into a slope—which has some distinct advantages—you'll need to dig some dirt. For a 7-foot wall height, you can probably dig only 3½ feet, piling the dirt on the uphill side to be pushed back against the finished stone wall later. In ledge-rock country you could possibly find a stone ledge to build against, eliminating the need for digging and for one 60-foot wall, but it's not likely, though I've seen examples of it and did build a small house that way once. You'll probably want the north side to be the submerged one, leaving the lower-level doors to open on the south for warmth in winter.

A contractor with a track loader or even a backhoe can scoop out your lower level; a bulldozer will not leave the square-cut corners and vertical cut you need. Before you consider digging it out by hand, understand that you're dealing with 156 cubic yards of dirt, or 26 dump-truck loads. You may decide on a barn on top of the ground, after all.

If you excavate, get the wall up against the cut as quickly as you can to keep it from washing. This can be drystone, since there's dirt beyond to seal, done like a retaining wall. If you're building two levels of stone, it should be mortared, on a footing. Pitch the subterranean wall against the fill or use buttresses or interior walls to support it. Here's where I'd try to use huge stones, set in place with the bucket of a front loader or with a boom for speed. If you build only this one level of stone and use drystone for this north wall, you'll want to mortar the south wall and the ends where they're aboveground, so that means a footing.

You could lay the whole barn dry, but you'd have a drafty barn. I know of a small one in Arkansas that's built this way, out of the excellent ledge sandstone of the region. The flexings of the drystone work won't disturb the beams overhead if they're solid enough and firmly joined.

DRAIN MOISTURE

You'll get some moisture through the banked walls whether you lay dry or mortared stone, unless you use a vapor barrier. With a dirt or gravel floor, there's going to be dampness underfoot anyway, so I ditch or use pipe drains from near the banked wall and leave it without a vapor barrier. Ditches will need periodic cleaning, and pipe will have to be screened to stay clear.

The minute you cut into the hillside, you'll have mud or clay or both. I haul gravel and spread it a couple of inches thick right away to have a floor of sorts. You'll have to add gravel from time to time as it sinks and gets scattered.

Once you're up to the top of the first level, you must concern yourself with joisting such a big structure. With the ridge running

Figure 18-3. Drystone barn near St. Joe, Arkansas. These structures were often plastered on the inside to keep out drafts.

the long way—east and west—it's best to extend the joists north and south. I never like to span over 10 feet, so that means joists in four sections, with sleeper supports or summer beams in three places. These beams should be supported by piers themselves, on footings, between stalls. The piers should be 8 by 8 inches—reinforced concrete instead of stone, to save space. The summer beams should be at least 8 by 12 inches, supporting joists 12 inches high and at least 2 inches thick on 2-foot centers. All this is to carry a 2-inch overhead oak floor capable of holding up machinery or even livestock.

Anchor the joist ends and the sleepers on a ledge at least 4 inches wide in the stonework. This means your second level will be thinner, but with appropriate bracing walls or buttresses you can support an 8- to 12-inch wall for the necessary height. If yours is to be just a one-level stone wall, set a sill on top, spanning windows and doors, and lay the joists on that. Then build the upper level of wood.

SPANS

For the two-level stone barn wall, you'll need to span windows and doors with lintels, arches, or braced keystone spans. The upper-level end drive-through doors will be huge, and I wouldn't span them with stone. Gables were often of stone, with these large doors spanned, but that's putting a lot of weight up high, where it's hard to brace, and I don't advise it. Make the gables of wood, and paint them for preservation.

If yours is only one level of stone, you may want to extend the joists out over the south wall a couple of feet. The overhang looks good and helps shelter the doorways from the sun in summer but lets it warm this wall in winter. This overhang won't present any serious building problems once it's floored. The floor will provide the base for the wooden upper level of the structure, whether flush with the stone wall or extended.

BARN RAISING

Once the stonework is complete, you're ready for the barn raising. Call on all the friends you have, plus the casual acquaintances, and of course all the neighbors you're speaking to. With proper supervision, a phenomenal amount of work can be done by twenty to fifty people on a project like this. If you feel qualified, play director. If not, get someone who can. One person has to be in charge. I should warn that the host is responsible for liquid refreshments, although the helpers usually bring dinner. The cost can be considerable, and of course there is the danger of accident. But a barn raising is a kind of fun you'll not soon forget.

Have all the beams ready ahead of time and know what needs doing. I like to build the wooden parts of barns post-and-beam, and there are some good books on the subject, notably *The Timber Framing Book* by Stewart Elliot and Eugenie Wallas (Kittery Point, Me.: Housesmiths Press, 1977). Essentially, you use heavy uprights, but fewer of them than studs in a conventional stud wall. The uprights are mortised into sills at the bottom and plates at the top. Diagonal bracing supports them laterally. Outside walls are usually covered in clapboard or board-and-batten. Traditionally, even in country where the houses were log, barns, mills, schools, and churches were post-and-beam with sawn board siding.

BRACING THE STONE

As we said, a structure as large as this one needs some support for the wall length. Simple interior diagonal braces would help but would be in the way. Whether you build one or two levels of stone, interior walls make sense, with the necessary support a function of the wall. These can be stable partitions or whatever, but you should have two or three of them in the 60-foot length of the wall, and at least one each along the 40-foot end walls.

Overhead joisting should follow the same pattern as that for the lower level, with uprights directly over the supporting piers below to carry the summer beams. And of course you'll need several lengths of beam to reach the 60 feet, spliced or half-notched and pinned. I recall a historic log barn in Ohio that had one-piece 60-feet hewn top plates, 16 inches square, of white oak, but you won't find anything like that today.

The roof design is up to you, although most people prefer the

Figure 18-4. A stone barn is a gigantic undertaking, but it will stand for generations as a monument to your farming.

gambrel for more storage space. It's built around a square framework of beams with the break in the roof at the top corners of the square. Cover the roof with whatever you can afford. Aluminum or galvanized iron is most common today, though shingles were used for hundreds of years in one form or another. I personally wouldn't want to shingle a large barn.

The big decision in building a stone barn is whether to go up above one level with the stone or not. Considering the labor, time, and quantity of stone required, I'd repeat what I said earlier about the availability of enough stone. Certainly the barn will last longer if it's all stone, even to the gable ends if properly braced against shifting beams or possible falling trees. Such a barn would be a monument, requiring more of your life than you probably would want to give it.

A barn of any size is a huge undertaking and if you build one at all, you may want a much smaller one. Certainly you'd stand a better chance of building a small one, say 24 by 32 feet, by yourself in a bearable time. You wouldn't be able to put much inside it, but it would serve for a couple of cows, some hay, and your tractor.

You might not even want it set into the ground, in which case building it would follow the lines of a dwelling house, without the frills. A drive-through or breezeway is still a good idea, with stables or stalls on each side.

Whatever your needs, a barn will become the focal point of your homestead, the place everything revolves around. So whether it's just a shed for your milk cow or big enough for a county-wide square dance, go at it thoughtfully and do it right.

Your great-grandchildren and their cows will be grateful.

Figure 19-1. Sometimes restoration has to begin with demolition, as with this chimney being pulled down as we took later additions off the Page Meadows log house. Chimneys are startlingly easy to topple.

CHAPTER NINETEEN

RESTORATION

RESTORING STONEWORK may be as simple as pointing up sections where mortar has fallen out or as involved as tearing out whole walls and rebuilding them. One of the most common restoration jobs is straightening up a stone fireplace chimney that has settled and leaned away from the house. Another is dismantling stonework at the original site to rebuild the structure in another place (Fig. 19-1).

Although stones are not recycled as readily as logs in a cabin, they can be reused, with a cleaning job to get the old mortar off. Usually the stones in an old structure are better, either because they've been chosen from a more abundant supply or because they've been cut and shaped to that structure. As we said in Chapter Three, a big prybar will get you a lot of usable material from old stonework.

POINTING UP

Let's look at the easy restoration jobs first. "Pointing up" is simply replacing mortar in structurally solid stonework. The old lime-and-sand mortar weathered away over a period of time, as did clay filling. If this weathering leaves enough mortar to hold the wall stable, repair is just a matter of getting new masonry mortar into the cracks and brushing it afterward.

Rake out crumbly mortar to a depth of 1 inch or more. Blow or brush out loose dust and sand first, and use a fine spray of water to dampen the crack you're about to fill. Do this just before filling, so the dry stone won't absorb moisture from the mortar. The small amount that a narrow crack requires will dry up quickly, leaving you with a crumbly fill no better than that you're replacing. Don't use so much water that the mortar runs, however.

Get a little strip of mortar on the bottom edge of the trowel and push it into the crack with a wiping, smearing action. With practice, pointing up will become a job you can do fairly fast.

Use the pointing tool here to wipe the mortar off the trowel and into the crack a strip at a time. This tool can also be used to rake the joint when partially set up to make it neat.

REPLACING STONES

Stones are sometimes completely loose, which is often the case over decayed wooden window and door lintels. The first thing to do is replace the lintel, if any. Then scrape out loose or crumbly mortar so that you have space all around the stone. Now "butter" the stone the way a brick mason does, putting mortar on all sides in this case, and push it back into place. Use enough mortar for a tight fit, so that some gets squeezed out to trim off. Point up, and then brush after four or five hours or when crumbly. To replace several stones that have fallen out, re-lay them (or replacements) from the bottom, then wedge in the top one or two as we just outlined.

Pointing up will just about always mean a mismatch in mortar joints. To avoid glaring evidence of what will look like a patch job, rake out all the joints in the wall and point it all up, whether it needs it structurally or not. A hay hook or something shaped like one works well for this.

Since you can't very well cover vertical pointing-up with sheet plastic to keep it moist, you'll have to do it another way or it will dry and then fall out. After you've brushed it, wet with a fine spray several times a day to keep enough moisture in the mortar to cure. Don't use enough water to run it or wash it out, but keep it visibly wet for three or four days. You will see masons totally ignoring this necessary moisture for curing, and you may be sure that you're watching today's get-the-money-and-run techniques.

WALL REPAIR

If a section of wall has fallen down, check the standing portion for soundness. Leaning, fractured stones and sagging or cracked joints mean you'll have to tear out more wall. A crack means there was stress at this point, and it may or may not have been relieved. If it's otherwise sound, you can chip or rake out the mortar from the cracked joint and point up. If the wall is still settling, it'll crack again.

Make sure there's solid footing under the part of the wall you're rebuilding. Chances are if it's an old wall the standing part has settled all it's going to, so build the restoration work on a reinforced footing, tying it into the existing wall.

If the break is more or less vertical, tear out more stones to make a stepped joint, to better tie the old work with the new. If you have to replace stones, try to match them with the same kind and size of stone, preferably with a similar weathered look.

A good way to join new work to old is to use $3/8$-inch reinforcing rod horizontally in the mortar joints between the two sections (Fig. 19-2). Chip or drive a hole in the old mortar, then extend about half a 12-inch piece out and enclose it with the new work.

Figure 19-2. You can tie rebuilt sections of stone wall to the original part with lengths of reinforcing rod mortared into the joints.

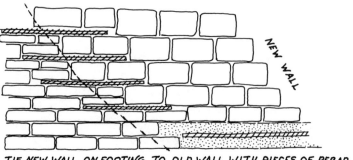

TIE NEW WALL, ON FOOTING, TO OLD WALL WITH PIECES OF REBAR

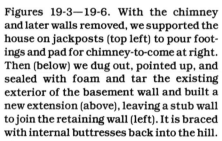

Figures 19-3—19-6. With the chimney and later walls removed, we supported the house on jackposts (top left) to pour footings and pad for chimney-to-come at right. Then (below) we dug out, pointed up, and sealed with foam and tar the existing exterior of the basement wall and built a new extension (above), leaving a stub wall to join the retaining wall (left). It is braced with internal buttresses back into the hill.

MATCH STYLE

On restoration work, stand back often to make sure what you're doing fits in with the whole. Each mason has his own style, as distinctive as a signature, and you're trying to work the way someone else did instead of the way you naturally do. When you finish the replacement section, recess the old mortar joints and point up the old work too, with the same mortar mix, to further tie the work visually. See Figs. 19-7—19-11.

Figures 19-7—19-11. This old stone building entryway (far left) has been filled in with plywood and some recent stonework at the left. First step in building an arched stone entryway was to tear out the plywood and framing. Stones were broken with a sledgehammer (upper left) and then chipped out on either side to provide anchoring ledges for the arch. Recycled reinforcing rod is bent (above) to shape in the blacksmith shop. Two bars are bent, then short lengths are welded between. The arch frame is propped in place (left) and stones laid up from either end. The frame must stay in place until the keystone is set and the mortar hardens partially. Then the rest of the stone can be laid. The completed arch (right) of creekbed limestone blends with the older stonework. The building is in the historic district of Hollister, Missouri, where all structures are of English-style and half-timber.

LEANING CHIMNEY

A tilting chimney is caused by the ground's softening out from the protection of the house, so it settles more on this side and leans. The more it leans, the more weight is concentrated on the outside, and the more it settles.

Usually the ground packs to a point of stability and the chimney stops tilting, sometimes before it falls over, sometimes not. This packing provides the one bright spot in a job of chimney-straightening, which usually means almost a complete razing and rebuilding. With the ground compressed so that even a tilting chimney is stable, it's plenty solid for a straight one, which won't put that extra strain on the outside edge.

So you can avoid having to dig everything out and pouring a new footing slab. I suppose if you left the chimney down for a long period, the ground might loosen up somewhat, but not much. The usual problem is that early builders didn't put enough stone down deep and wide. The tilting, settling chimney packed it down to a point of stability in time. At ground level you can compensate for the slope with a layer of slightly tapered stones (where it won't show) to get plumb again, then rebuild from there on up.

RECORD IT FIRST

Before you tear out any stonework, photograph it with something better than a quickie idiot camera. To have a visual model to work toward, get a good, sharp negative you can enlarge or a color slide you can project.

I have photographed several complete houses to document for restoration, including an 1850s cabin for a doctor friend in Harrison, Arkansas, who had it dismantled, moved, and completely restored, working entirely from the pictures. It became a model frontier doctor's office on his farm.

You can also number or code stones in a chimney, but lay them out over a wide area when rebuilding so you can find them again, and don't use chalk or any medium that rubs or washes off easily. If you count on just the code, make measurements and notes on mortar joint size and major dimensions.

ONE AT A TIME

When you dismantle a chimney or anything built of stone, you cannot be too careful. If you have a pile of sand or sawdust below, you can drop one stone at a time onto it after you've carefully pried them off. If not, then each stone should be taken down with the same care you use in getting stones up when building. A front loader is handy here, or a forklift with pallets for the stones.

Most chimney restorations are carried out with regard only for the general size and shape of stones, and each stone is not put back in the exact space it came from. In a given chimney there will be many stones almost the same, and these can be scrambled with little harm. In cases of shoulder stones where a chimney narrows, or a fireplace face, or mantel stones, care should be taken to replace them exactly, and here is where the photographs are handy.

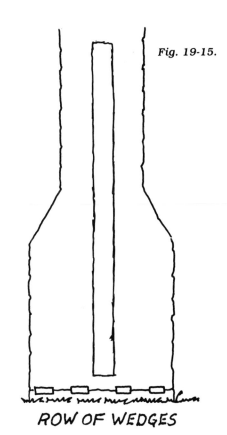

Fig. 19-13.

LAY NEW STONE IN CRACK OR WEDGE IN PIECES OF IRON WITH MORTAR

ROW OF WEDGES

Fig. 19-14.

Fig. 19-15.

STRAIGHTENING A CHIMNEY

There is another way to straighten a tilted chimney, but I hesitate to outline it because it is both difficult and quite dangerous. It is quicker than razing and rebuilding, however, so here goes:

First, get a hard hat. Then box in the chimney with a close-fitting wooden structure, or crate, to keep stones from jarring loose and falling. Or wrap it in heavy canvas and lash with rope. Next, dig a short V-shaped ditch about 15 feet away, crossways. Now lay a timber in the ditch on the slope away from the chimney. Set another heavy timber, at least 4 inches thick, vertically against the chimney. Lay a push beam up against this one, to reach almost to the ditch, blocked about 8 feet up the vertical one, so it can't creep up. Find the biggest hydraulic jack in the country (20 tons or so) and set it up firmly between the push beam and the one in the ditch. See Fig. 19-12.

Apply pressure carefully to take out all the slack. Make sure the push beam is straight, square-cut at the ends, and secure. Now start a half dozen wedges—which can be stone chisels or even timber wedges—into the mortar joint nearest the ground on the outside of the chimney (Figs. 19-14, 19-15). Tap them in until they're firm, then apply a little more pressure on the jack. Tap some more, one wedge at a time. They'll be hard to get started, so dig some mortar out first.

ROW OF WEDGES

Figures 19-12—19-15. A chimney can be straightened this way with care. Wedges are driven as force is applied to the push beam. Then the crack is filled with thin stones or iron pieces mortared in.

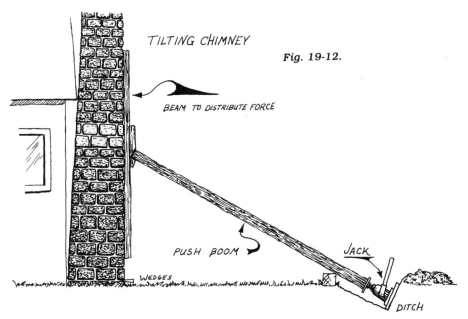

TILTING CHIMNEY

Fig. 19-12.

BEAM TO DISTRIBUTE FORCE

PUSH BOOM

JACK

WEDGES

DITCH

BRUTE FORCE

More pressure, more wedging. Eventually the chimney will start to move and the crack will widen. Keep at it until the chimney is vertical again.

Now leave the jack in place and knock out maybe two wedges for some space to work. Clean the mortar out and push in new tapered stones, buttered all around with mortar, if there's room. If there's no room for stones, drive in flat pieces of iron and work mortar all around them. Be sure to fill the entire crack, to take the weight better. Remove two more wedges and repeat. See Fig. 19-13.

I like to leave the two outside wedges till last and work from the inside. Then I let the new mortar cure before I knock these out. This way, if the beam slips, either the wedges or the cured stonework/iron will hold the chimney. After all the stone is in, I let it stand

Figure 19-16. Tilled stone chimney at Turnback Mill house, built in 1859. The space behind has been partially filled with brick, visible at the bottom of the photograph.

for a week, then let the jack down. Very slowly.

This is one of those projects that sounds easier than it is. In practice, the jack or beam may slip. The wedges will certainly crush the stone against them, so you may want to use maple or some other hardwood for wedges after you've started a crack. Certainly the jack's mechanism will let pressure leak off, so nudge the handle now and then to keep tension on; or, better, replace with a longer push beam on each side of it, so you can let them take the strain and give the jack a rest.

If, God forbid, all that wedging and propping should give way and the chimney start to fall, do not philosophize or conjecture. Set a new speed record away from there!

And unless you have worked in heavy construction a great deal, don't even attempt this method. It will work, but it's the sort of undertaking that you can't afford a goof-up on. It's safer but more laborious to take the chimney apart and rebuild it. Of course, if the mortar joints are weak anyway, it should be dismantled and rebuilt regardless.

OLD CHIMNEYS OFTEN LEAN

I've seen chimneys anchored to the house with iron bands. This was done by initial builders to forestall tilting, but in some cases the bands were probably added after restoration work, to keep it from happening again. A footing deep and wide enough won't let the chimney tilt in the first place, but it's hard to anticipate the thrust of so many tons of stone concentrated on so small an area.

It was common practice to build the chimney up against the house but not joined to it, so that the settling would allow the chimney to slide down. A crack or evidence of a crack's having been filled at the mantel indicates that this settling has occurred.

CRACKED STONES

When rebuilding a fireplace and chimney, you'll nearly always find a cracked lintel or other stones cracked from heat if not from settling. With no insulation in the older houses, folks built big fires to fight the chill. And fire next to stone has never been a good idea, as you'll recall from crackling campfires you've known.

Replacing an important stone like a lintel or a keystone will mean some stone cutting and shaping. And of course the new work will look new, so you might want to sandblast old stone around it for uniformity. It's harder to age the new work, although you can cut it, then lay it outdoors face up, wetting it often for a few months while the sun, leaf mold, and dirt do what they can to age it. Better to avoid cutting or shaping the outward surface at all, so its weathered look will match more closely.

Figures 19-17—19-21. The stone chimney at Page Meadows before restoration (near right) during other work. We removed the old brick top, typical in central Virginia, and (below) rebuilt the stone shoulder and brick work. Then Mike Firkaly (middle right) picked out the smeared lime-and-sand mortar for repointing. The difference is that of good dry work made sloppy (far right) and made to look good again. The finished chimney and house are below, right. The stone chimney had replaced a brick one on the original late 1700s structure during a major overhaul of the house in 1859-1860.

WOOD AGAINST STONE

Wood was used by our ancestors in altogether too many places to brace stonework. Often a window lintel was no more than a 2x4 down flat, with a flat span over it and no keystone (somebody grabbed the money and ran then, too). And often you'll find small cracks, or even large ones, showing that the stones have settled. You're better off to repair this type of problem area by first replacing the lintel with angle-iron bracing, or change to a keystone span. In most cases you won't want to change from a flat span to an arch, though this would solve the problem.

We mentioned loose facings in Chapter Nine. If the wood is good, the best restoration is the simplest. Bore new holes in the wood, countersinking, then bore holes in the mortar with a masonry bit. Use anchor bolts to firm up the facings, and fill the countersunk heads with a filler or glue in a wooden peg.

If the wood is bad or if the mortar is too far gone to anchor bolts, take everything out, including about 3 inches of mortar. Then set anchor bolts with 90-degree bends in them into the joints and mortar around them as with pointing up. Be sure to work it back into the spaces well, using a rod to work out all the air. Then bore holes in new facings, countersink them, and bolt up when the mortar is cured.

BROKEN WALL

Another common repair for stone structures results from the fracture made by a tree growing at the base of a wall. Usually the crack will run up and around the stones in the mortar, but some stones may be broken. The roots will go down, then under the wall.

First of all, the tree must be taken out. It will continue to grow and break the wall again if left in. Then the stump must be grubbed out, which is quite a job if it's a big tree. You can dig down to each root and chop it, then pull the weakened stump with a come-along. If the come-along won't pull it, use a sheave for a snatch block to double your pull and try again (Fig. 19-22). If it still won't budge, dig some more and chop some more.

Once out, you'll have a hole or holes where the stump and roots were. Take out everything solid and dig out all loose dirt. You may find that the wall settles after a few days, closing the cracks. If so, pour concrete into the hole to fill it up to the bottom of the wall. Then you can chip or rake out mortar along the crack and point up again. If broken stones have weakened the wall too much, chip away the mortar, rake it out with the hay hook, and remove the broken pieces. Then fit new stones into the holes. See Fig. 19-23.

If the wall is heaved clear out of line and doesn't settle back with removal of the stump, you'll have to dig both ways up and down the wall to remove dirt that has washed in as the tree pushed it up. When you've taken out all that seems to be holding up the wall, bump it with a heavy section of log—gently at first, to shake it and let it settle. Don't hit it hard enough to start any more cracks. If the wall is pushed out of line laterally, this will help get it back (hit it on the outside of the bulge).

If vines and dirt have filled the fracture itself, dig and wash it out before you try to settle the wall. If you get it back in place, pour a footing with some steel rod in it into the space you dug out.

If all efforts to settle the wall fail, go ahead and pour concrete under it, chip out along the fracture, replace broken stones, and point up. Then take out just the top course that is out of line, blocking up any structure on top of it (if it's a foundation wall), and lay new stone to level it up. With the concrete footings you've poured, the new level will stay put.

Another way is to dig out the stump and any dirt that seems to be holding up the raised part of the wall, then leave everything alone for a few weeks. Keep folks away just in case you've dug out too much and the wall falls—which is unlikely, since you'll have left the ground undisturbed away from the stump area. In time the wall should settle by itself. Give it a thump now and then to let it know you haven't forgotten it.

If the fractures or settling cracks aren't too bad, just leave them. The wall will adjust to the change slowly and remain pretty stable, particularly in the case of settling. After you get the tree out you may not have a wall bad enough to warrant digging out, re-settling, re-footing, and pointing up. Large cracks aren't so good, but the friction still at work in a fine fracture will give lots of inertia to your wall.

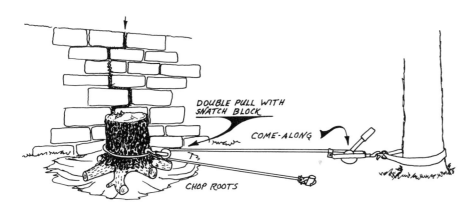

Figure 19-22. Pulling the stump of a tree that has broken a stone wall. The snatch block doubles the pull of the cable ratchet hoist. More leverage can be obtained if the stump is left taller and the cable attached higher.

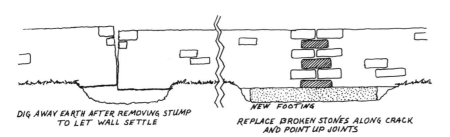

DIG AWAY EARTH AFTER REMOVING STUMP TO LET WALL SETTLE

REPLACE BROKEN STONES ALONG CRACK AND POINT UP JOINTS

Figure 19-23. Replace broken stones and pour a concrete footing under the wall where the stump was. You may have to dig out more to let the wall settle back into place.

DRYSTONE RESTORATION

Restoration of drystone structures is in some ways more difficult, mainly because you can't take out a stone without having the ones above it shift. You have to take out a whole V-shaped section, which is a mess if there's a building on top of the wall. Study the structure and locate points where wedges can be driven to take the weight from above, lifting slightly to let you remove and replace, or just tighten, the offending stones (Fig. 19-24). If a section is poorly laid and has fallen out, you may need to go all the way up to repair it. If it's a foundation, work heavy steel beams through under the sill and raise with jacks on both sides to let you make the repairs (Fig. 19-25). Raise just an inch or so at a time, to let the building adjust itself.

Always build drystone repaired sections up a bit higher than the already settled parts so that everything will come back down even. A half inch or so is enough. If the new part settles a bit more or less, it won't be noticeable. If laid up even, the new part won't ever take its share of the weight.

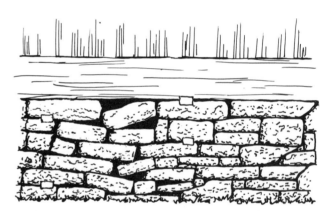

WEDGE UP DRY STONES TO REPAIR OR REPLACE
WEAK PORTION

HOLD SILL UP WITH JACKS
TO REPAIR STONEWORK

Figures 19-24 and 19-25. To replace dry stonework under a sill, wedge up or use an I-beam and jacks to raise the structure while you rebuild the wall.

Figures 19-26—19-28. Strengthening and sealing a drystone basement wall begins with excavation (top left) to below floor level. Then dirt is brushed from stones, forms built and reinforced concrete poured, which is sealed with polyurethane foam (above). Drain tile with gravel fill to help keep the basement dry. The wall is pointed up inside (left) and the job is complete.

BEWARE!

Everything I said about watching for uglies in the chapter on acquiring stone goes double for working with drystone structures. There are proportionately many more holes and hiding places for crawlies than among stones scattered at random in their wild state.

I was working with my friend Bill Cameron on the Turnback Creek gristmill restoration (Figs. 19-29—19-31) one August day a few years back. The old drystone foundation was 6 feet high on the creek side and a good 2 feet thick, two stones with tie stones across and lots of odd spaces inside. Working with crosscut saw over a particular area, we'd fitted sills for the mill framing on the pegged lap joints. Now we were laying out the heavy floor joists, and at sunset I was cutting off the uneven ends of the oak with a chainsaw at the same spot.

I caught a glimpse of movement from under the newly laid sill and immediately suspected a snake. Bill said yes, he'd seen something there earlier, thought it was a mouse. Just then up came the large head and 8 inches of a copperhead, bigger than any I'd seen. It couldn't seem to get out now that we'd laid the sill. And both of us had been stepping over that thing all day, filtering sawdust down on it, bumping the big sills into place. Bill was a still-spry seventy-seven that year, but not spry enough to step on a snake and get off again before it could bite him.

SCORCHED STONE TECHNIQUE

We thought about leaving it, but we knew one of us would indeed step on it there or somewhere else around the job. We reluctantly sloshed a little chainsaw gas down the hole and lit it. Amid the flames and thrashing inside, a head would poke out here or there and then recede while we waited in horrible suspense with a couple of long sticks. Finally out it came, like a small alligator, as big as my arm.

But with all those joists across we couldn't get a good swat at it, and off it crawled toward the creek side of the foundation. Bill ran around to head it off, but it was gone. Cooling itself in the creek, we supposed.

Getting dark then. I checked around to make sure there were no others and doused the fire. Then I started the chainsaw for the last few cuts before we quit. Halfway through the next-to-last joist, up came about half that snake over the last joist, obviously irritated.

For a wild moment I considered trying to slice it to bits with the chainsaw but didn't have the nerve (also, I got a mental picture of hooking its tough skin and whipping it back all over me). So I deliberately set the chainsaw aside, shut it off with exaggerated calm, then sailed about 20 feet off the stone wall.

Scared the snake, too. It went back under the creekside sill and lay there, while Bill, a realist, went to borrow a gun. It took several minutes, but the snake just lay there, a silhouette in the dying light in a space between the stone wall and the joist above it.

Well, the neighbors had a .410 shotgun with one shell in it, which Bill brought. It was so dark only a glint from the faintly red sky showed me which way the gun barrel was pointed, but I let fly anyway from as close as I wanted to get, which wasn't close. Blew a chunk out of the rock, and I suppose the rock fragments plus the shock got the snake. Anyway, we were able to make several pieces of it with an axe.

The next day a state conservation agent who dropped by said 42 inches was the record copperhead and that it sounded like this was as big or bigger. Bill chided me with his Irish twinkle, saying I should have measured the snake before I shot it.

MILL TAKES LOTS OF STONE

We did a lot of stonework on that restoration. We kept the dry-stone foundations intact but built others of mortared work. That's rocky country, but the best stones had been used a century before for the mill, mill dam, millrace, and the 1850s house. I couldn't match the fine drystone work with the rock I had.

Figure 19-29. Bill Cameron and my brother John, at work with some of the stones from a nearby barn foundation, on the Turnback Mill restoration in 1975. We joined the new walls to the old with steel rods mortared into the joints.

Bill had a friend a few miles away who'd just torn down a decayed barn he'd built half a century earlier and now was giving us the stones for the mill. My brother John helped haul these, and he enjoyed the reminiscences of the old gentleman.

"Hauled all these rocks in here myself with a wagon and team," he said, his eyes somewhere beyond the brush-grown fields and on the young man he had once been. Some of the stones were pretty big, and John, who's a muscular man himself, needed help with them.

"You handled them all yourself? That was quite a job."

"Yep. Nobody else on the place. I remember right where most every one of 'em came from, even now."

There was one huge boulder down under the others, and John worked toward it, measuring it with practiced eye. No two men could have moved that rock around. The fellow talked on about the job.

"Had to roll some of 'em down a bank onto the wagon. Yes sir, moved 'em all myself."

John was down to the big one. "That one, now." He pointed. "You remember how that one got there, don't you?"

The old man peered. "That big 'un? Well, now. . ."

"That one was the one you built the barn around, wasn't it?"

"Well, now, you're sure right. I built 'er on that one right where she lays!" He was delighted at the memory.

"And the way I see it," my brother said, "somebody else can build another barn around it, 'cause I sure can't move it."

And maybe, in our own sure return to the earth and onto the grown-up farms again, and into the hills, someday somebody will.

LEGACY IN STONE

I love old stonework, whether it's the fallen, tree-grown, drystone work along an ancient field, or the ivy-covered perfection of a mansion from another era, or a mossy springhouse, or a keystoned bridge. In the houses I build, I always recycle stones when I can, and I enjoy reliving the long-ago days of those people who toiled to raise them the first time. Their joys, their labors, their bornings and dyings become a part of my house now, to live on at least in my memory and in my imagination.

Our house has a lot of recycled foundation stones, but it's the chimney-base stones I like. There was once a cabin deep in the most remote and beautiful part of the Buffalo River country in Arkansas, near Hemmed-in-Hollow. Here many of the sandstone blocks had curious, rounded hollows in them about 2 inches across. The early cabin builders had used several of these in their foundation and their chimney.

I stumbled onto the site years ago, when only a few scattered stones remained, and later I lifted some for the chimney I was to build for our house. They're now the first course of weathered

Figure 19-30. Bill Cameron mixes mortar for the Turnback Mill restoration. After I had begun the stonework and set the mill wheel bearings, he went on to complete the millrace, lining it with stone himself. The 13-foot wheel was set in the open space in the foreground.

sandstone in our chimney, with their distinctive pockmarks.

I lived for years in that country, with the kerosene lamps and the horse-drawn implements and the stony fields and the hardscrabble ways. Pioneer stones, you help me live again those long April twilights that smelled of turned earth and wildflowers and woodsmoke, veiled now in unreal romance. The long toil and the sudden mountain joys, sharp as a storm in summer, are still borne to me now by a few simple stones.

And I am grateful.

Figure 19-31. Bill Cameron with volunteer Mike Chiles and my daughter Amanda, now a teenager, at the completed Turnback millrace and wheel in late 1977. Bill died at 89, still active, still the best ''apprentice'' I ever had.

GLOSSARY

aggregate	Substance made up of different-sized particles, such as sand and gravel.
anchor bolts	Bolts set into masonry to anchor wooden or metal construction members.
annealed	Softened metal, to avoid breakage.
aqueduct	Man-made watercourse, often raised.
ash dump	In a fireplace, an opening for removal of ashes.
ashlar	Stone cut in regular straight-line patterns.
berm-type building	One built largely into the ground.
bond	Pattern of laying masonry to tie more than one thickness together.
boom	Extended beam for lifting.
breast wheel	Waterwheel with water entering buckets part way up.
breezeway	Open passage through house or barn.
buttering	In masonry, coating the brick or stone partially with mortar before laying it.
buttress	Short bracing portion of a wall, at right angles to it.
calcium chloride	Chemical that, when added to mortar, retards freezing.
cantilever	Portion of a structure extending horizontally, unsupported.
capstones	Those stones along the top of a wall.
catslide roof	Roof extending at an unbroken angle over added parts of a structure.
cement	Chemically bonding substance mixed with sand and/or gravel, for mortar or concrete.
chert	A limestone, often containing flint deposits.
chimney cap	Cover to keep rain, birds, leaves out.
"come along"	Ratchet cable or chain hoist.
concrete	Mixture of cement, sand, gravel, and water to form a solid material.
curing	In mortar or concrete, keeping wet until the chemical action is complete.
damper	Device for restricting passage of air or smoke up a chimney.
double-glaze	To construct a window of two layers of glass.
drystone	Construction of stone with no mortar.
dry wall	Plasterboard wall covering.
duct	Enclosed passage, usually for heated or cooled air.
English bond	A pattern in brickwork alternating a row of lengthwise bricks with a row of crosswise ones to bond two thicknesses together.
face rocks	Those covering the face of a wall, as in veneer.
facings	Door or window framing.
fieldstone	Stone, found on top of the ground, used in its naturally occurring shapes.
fill	Loose earth placed in a depression to achieve height.

firebox	A usually metal enclosure for containing fire and radiating heat.
firebrick	A heat-resistant brick for use next to fire.
flagstone	Thin stone used as a floor or walkway.
flashing	Thin metal sheeting used to seal joints in buildings against rain.
flat keystone span	A self-supporting horizontal span formed of shaped stones.
Flemish bond	Pattern in brickwork alternating a lengthwise brick with a crosswise one to tie two thicknesses together.
flue	Enclosed vertical passage for smoke.
flue tile	Ceramic lining used in chimneys.
flume	Open-top trough for flowing water.
footing	Base for a structure or wall foundation.
forms	Temporary shaping structures for pouring concrete.
gambrel roof	One with a convex angle in the slope about halfway up.
gin poles	Pair of beams forming an A shape for lifting.
girt	Beam across a structure to brace opposite sides.
green mortar	That which is hard but not cured.
grid	Crisscross patten forming squares, as of reinforcing rods.
header	Stone or brick laid with its short end outward.
heat exchanger	Device for extracting heat, replacing with cold.
heaved ground	That swelled from water frozen in it.
hillside cut	A bank resulting from vertical digging.
hydraulic ram	Water-powered pump for transporting water.
joists	Timbers on which a floor or ceiling is laid.
keystone	That stone in a span which locks the others in place.
keystone span	Structure bridging an opening, held with a keystone.
king post	Timber bracing a joist from a ridge peak.
knee wall	Low upstairs vertical wall under a roof slope.
ledge pattern	Flat stones laid horizontally in a structure.
lichens	Moisture-nourished organic growths on stones.
lintel	A single stone spanning an opening.
loft	Open space above the ceiling, enclosed by the roof.
masonry cement	Cement and lime mix, for bonding stonework.
masonry sealer	Varnish-like substance for sealing masonry against water.
mason's hammer	One with a chisel-like extension for shaping stones.
millrace	Channel for water to a mill wheel.
mortar	Bonding substance of cement, sand, and water.
mortared construction	Masonry bonded with mortar, as opposed to dry-stone work.
''mud''	Mason's slang for mortar.
multiple keystone	A type of span utilizing several shaped stones to distribute the wedging function of the keystone.
muriatic acid	Commercial hydrochloric acid, used diluted to clean stonework.
overshot wheel	A mill wheel over which water is channeled for power.
pintles	One-piece hinge pins and mountings.

pitching tool	Stone chisel with one surface flat and the opposite beveled, for removing protrusions.
plate	Horizontal beam across the top of a wall to support the roof.
plumb bob	Pointed weight on a string for maintaining vertical level.
pointing up	In masonry, filling cracks between stones or bricks with mortar.
Poncelet wheel	An undershot mill wheel having curved, open blades to extract more force from the water.
portland cement	Unmixed cement used in concrete, originally from Portland, England.
quarry	Natural deposit of stone from which stone is cut and removed.
queen posts	Double vertical beams braced by a cross beam under the roof peak, used to brace joists or rafters.
random pattern	Stonework consisting of uneven shapes and sizes, with vertical joints covered.
reinforced concrete	That having steel rods or mesh inside for strength.
reinforcing rods	Steel rods for strengthening concrete.
riser	The vertical face of a step.
roof trusses	Units consisting of rafters and braces, self-supporting.
rubble	Stonework consisting of stones of all sizes and shapes with no effort made at any pattern; also, broken waste stone.
sap	Moisture in newly quarried stone.
scaffold	Temporary structure for working high areas of a wall.
screed	Board for leveling newly poured concrete, as for a floor.
setting up	The hardening of concrete or mortar.
sheave	Pulley used with rope or cable.
shoulder stones	In a chimney, those at the point of the chimney's narrowing.
sills	Horizontal beams on a foundation upon which a building rests.
slab	In masonry construction, a wide concrete base for a structure; also, a concrete floor.
sleeper	Support beam on which joists are laid.
smoke shelf	Horizontal ledge inside a chimney to retard downdrafts.
snatch block	A sheave or pulley used to multiply the force of a pull by rope or cable.
spillway	Overflow of a dam.
stoneboat	Sled used for moving stones.
stone course	A horizontal layer of stone in a wall.
stone point	A tool used for fine shaping of stone.
stretcher	Lengthwise stone in a wall, paralleling it.
struck joints	Mortar between stones shaped or brushed while soft or crumbly.
stud wall	Wall or type of construction of multiple light vertical timbers.
submersible pump	One that is entirely covered by the liquid it pumps.
subsoil	That below the topsoil, usually of clay or other nonorganic material.
summer beam	A sleeper, or horizontal joist support.
tie stone	One that extends across a wall of more than one stone thickness.

torque	Twisting force.
tread	The horizontal surface of a step.
trowel	Tool for applying or spreading mortar.
turbine	Advanced, enclosed hydraulic wheel producing power.
undershot wheel	Waterwheel utilizing flow of stream along its lower edge.
urea-formaldehyde foam	Plastic insulation material.
vapor barrier	Waterproof layer in construction to seal out moisture.
vermiculite concrete	That with vermiculite mixed into it, to trap air pockets for insulation.

INDEX

Illustrations are in bold; Margin notes are in italics.